THE TERROR OF ILLUSION

A Dialogue with Crisula Stefanescu

BY

AUGUSTIN BUZURA

THE TERROR OF ILLUSION

A Dialogue with Crisula Stefanescu

BY

AUGUSTIN BUZURA

Translated from the Romanian by Delia Dragulescu

East European Monographs, Boulder, Colorado

DISTRIBUTED BY COLUMBIA UNIVERSITY PRESS, NEW YORK

2007

East European Monographs, No. DCCXIII

ISBN: 978-0-88033-611-6
Library of Congress Control Number: 2007935633

Printed in the United States of America

The Terror of Illusion

Crisula Stefanescu: *You have been in the West for almost two months now and we have talked to each other many times, but unfortunately we did not record our conversations. You came here feeling tired, stressed, spiritually in a dilemma, at a crossroads, wishing to have some time for yourself, to step away from everything and reflect on the things that were essential to you.*

Augustin Buzura: When one finds oneself in a stressful situation, one considerably limits one's horizon. That is why I wanted to come here, I wanted to detach myself from those stressful conditions in order to be able to think about what I had done and about what I would have to do hereafter, apart from what I should write about, in order to stop and consider if what I was doing was rightly done. I also wanted to find out which were the topics people in the West wrote about nowadays. Where was literature heading to.

C.S.: *Ideologically unconditioned.*

A.B.: Unconditioned in any way. These two past months have been incredibly important for me. It has been like some kind of a re-meditation phase, of rethinking everything I thought about at home, in Romania. It has been a confirmation of the fact that I was right to detach myself in order to have a better view. I wanted to analyse myself, the person I am today, to see how I have evolved, which were my resolutions about literature and about the world I live in, about everything in general. I rethought every idea, every obsession, every preoccupation I have ever had. Being alone, living isolated, just me and my self, I could analyse everything again. This period of detachment was very useful to me, as I did not trouble about what I ate, what I wore, how to get rid of the cold and of all my worries. Furthermore, I had a chance to talk to various people. I wanted to find out how they saw the world, how they saw history.

C.S.: *I understand that you are at a crossroads, a moment when you want to or must make a choice.*

A.B.: Exactly. I have to choose between being useful to the moment or being useful to literature.

C.S.: *Maybe it would be better to serve them both at the some time...*

A.B.: This is precisely what I want. This is what I am thinking about, how to reconcile both of them. The thought of having to give one of them up by making a choice, is excruciating, I feel it like a fierce pain.

C.S.: *Marin Sorescu stated somewhere, and I have to admit that I have never thought about it before, that in your novels there was almost no physical pain, but there was a more fierce, overwhelming, mental pain: the pain of powerlessness.*

A.B.: I think the absence of physical pain from my novels derives from my former occupation, that of a doctor. From a literary point of view, it would be too easy for me to describe it. And it always seemed unimportant to me as well. I do not know why, but I was always certain that physical pain was not essential. Sorescu's observation has never crossed my mind either. I did not deliberately eliminate physical pain from my books. Not intentionally, but instinctively. In most cases, physical pain can be cured. But today, there is almost nothing we can do about moral pain.

C.S.: *That is true. It is a more exciting theme. I have noticed that you are against imposed themes in literature, and I believe you are quite right. However, don't you think that some themes are imposed on us by the historical circumstances?*

A.B.: Yes, absolutely. I have always been dreaming about universally human themes that live beyond the moment, but unfortunately, history and the times that we endure imposed their themes on me. I finally found a compromise. I thought that the relationship between man and history, between man and environment, could also be built by using the material put forward by history. For instance, I thought that the Bible, which is first of all a history, the history of the Jewish people told by various prophets from different perspectives, or the New Testament, the history of Christ and of his apostles, could both be read as histories or interpreted as parables or as prophecies. I thought that the important thing was knowing how to choose from what one had inside or around oneself that which could go beyond the moment of choice, that which would have or would acquire a universally human significance. But this is a late discovery of mine. At the beginning, I would let myself be lead by the need of immediately responding to a certain event. And, if it had turned out the way I had dreamt of and I had become a journalist, I believe that first, I would not have written as many books as I did, and second, what I would have written would have looked differently. In the end, I came to the conclusion that I had to be a bit of a journalist as well, and I started writing what was called *Notebook*, which helped me transfer some of my nervous energy in a different place, so that the text of the prose could be liberated from the explosive charge of the moment.

C.S.: *The literary critics did not pay much attention to* Notebook.

A.B.: On the one hand, the critics, with a few exceptions, were not that interested in social issues. On the other hand, in other cases, it was a tacit agreement. The readers were left to discover those issues on their own. Maybe you noticed that the critics had not analysed the main subject of any of my books. Sometimes intentionally, they looked for a secondary theme to focus on, in order to give me the possibility to have other books published as well.

C.S.: *In* Notebook, *you wrote almost obsessively about miners. Why? Generally, the narrative of your novels takes place in an urban environment and nevertheless, in your last novel,* The Road of The Ash, *you expressed moving realities about peasants. Did you ever think of writing a novel with and about them?*

A.B.: Strangely enough, my first thought was to write about them, about peasants. I even debuted with a story about peasants. It was the environment I knew best. I am referring to the peasants in Maramures, but there is not much difference between them and other peasants. At that time, I thought that I had to write only about what I knew closely. I had actually lived both in the peasants' and miners' environment, and for the past thirty years I have been living in the intellectuals' environment. My father worked in a mine. In the mines on Dealul Crucii. Then he worked at "Phoenix", the lead factories in Baia Mare, where he was a founding worker. That is how he died, intoxicated with lead. He had a terribly complicated life.

C.S.: *Have you ever thought of reconstructing it?*

A.B.: No, I have never thought about it. He never spoke about what had happened in his life, and therefore, it was more of a legend to me.

C.S.: *What memories do you have from your childhood?*

A.B.: Oh, it was a really strange time for me. The first thing I remember is related to the war. My father came home from the factory and said: "The war has started. Baia Mare is full of refugees." This is my first memory from my childhood, these are the first words I recall. Afterwards, a frightening period started. My father was sent to forced labour by Horthy's troops, because that part of Transylvania had been conceded to Hungary. He was sent to digging tranches, somewhere 15 km away from the village. I even remember having seen my father literally drawing the yoke. The peasants were wearing no shirts and were covered in blood. The land was ploughed by the peasants drawing the yoke. It was aimed at intimidating the population. This is an image that was forever stamped in my mind and soul. This ishow history was written. I remember it because it is connected to the first images I have of my father.

I also remember that later my father would not sleep at home, for fear of not taking him away, of not picking him up. He would shortly come home and then he would disappear again. There had been a war going on for such a long time that we would not know anymore who was fighting who. I was living in fear, fear that was passed on to me by the grown-ups, fear that sometimes I can still sense today. The doors were always being locked with big keys, as country houses used to have. And well, it seems that even today I can still hear that noise. And then the war was over. The Russians came. The collectivisation started. My father was less exposed because he was part of the "working class". Therefore, the attic of our house filled with people. I remember the black cars of the *Securitate* driving around to take the village "kulaks" away. The priest slept in our attic for a long time. As many others did as well. Because the *Securitate* raids were taking place only during the night, we would take the ladder away in the evening and then put it back in the morning for them to go back to their homes.

C.S.: *What was your parents' religion?*

A.B.: My father was a Uniate, and my mother Orthodox.

C.S.: *And the priest?*

A.B.: There was something curious happening in our village. The priest, Gheorghe Ghetie, was holding sermons at both the

Orthodox and Uniate churches. I indirectly owe a lot to him. He used to live 50 m behind our house. He was a first-rate intellectual and, for as long as the *Securitate* searches lasted, he moved his entire library in our house. Therefore, I had the chance to read immensely during that time. The priest had another characteristic, and later, after I had studied psychiatry, I tried to understand him. His house, actually the courtyard of his house, was full of mentally ill people brought in from the entire country, from as far as Dobrogea. He used to take them to an old XVth century church.

C.S.: *Does it still exist?*

A.B.: No, it was a small church that, after having been declared historical monument, was abandoned and it was destroyed by a storm. So, the priest would take these people into the church at night, and he would read sermons to them. My father used to help him because the patients were taken there tied. And later, after having heard those sermons, they would come out on their two feet, I mean, they would not be tied anymore, but freed from evil spirits. The priest's land was neighbouring our land, and my mother was always frightened by his patients, and she used to tell me all the time to keep the door locked: "Be aware of the priest's crazy patients, not to do you any harm." This was my first contact with psychiatry.

C.S.: *How is it that you thought of studying psychiatry?*

A.B.: Oh, this is a decision I took much later. It has nothing to do with the priest and his crazy patients, although, when I became a doctor, I tried to reconstruct the patients' diagnoses based on my memories. I was able to explain some diagnoses, but not all of them. I remember an epileptic that was brought in tied to a wagon. Today, I would say that he was in status. He came back, let's say, "rehabilitated". It was a miracle. The priest was doing miracles. I believe that this is one of the reasons for which he was truly respected in our village. As any other true believer, he believed that God was the same for all, and so, he would make no difference between a Catholic and an Orthodox, that was not important to him.

C.S.: *What happened to the priest?*

A.B.: The priest died when I was in 3rd grade. There is another story which had haunted me for a long time, and it is also related to the priest. I think it was in October 1944 when the Russians came to our village. The Hungarians, the Hungarian army I mean, fled, and the people hid in the forest for fear of revenge and cruelties. We all ran away. We had a radio which ran on batteries, and we used to listen to BBC all the time. We did not understand much of it though. Someone would translate, but would do it in his own way, more by ear and by guessing. We would also listen to *Radio Bucuresti*, which sometimes had a pretty clear sound. We had stayed hidden in the forest until someone came and shouted that the Romanians were arriving, and then we all got out, with wagons, children, flags and banners, with all our belongings. My father, who just couldn't stay still for a moment, had gone to the village a few times before to check if the Hungarians were leaving, if the Romanians were coming. They even shot at him, but luckily he slipped the moment they fired, because otherwise he would not have escaped alive.

As I just said, we got out of the forest but instead of the Romanians we all expected to see, there were Russians! The Germans had installed cannons in our house, which was on top of a hill, and when they fled, they left them there, with ammunition and everything. The first Russian that came into the house, looked around and saw that the walls were full of icons, the old icons that can be found in Maramures. He had an automatic rifle and he fired at them all. This was my first contact with Russians. Then a few soldiers from Besssarabia came and they helped us talk to the Russians.

We did not have any place left to hide. The Russians would not use the roads anymore, but they would flow from all directions, from the hills, from the villages' side streets, hunting down the Germans and the Hungarians. We had tried to hide somewhere, but then we realised that it was useless, that we could not be safe anywhere, so we returned home. When we entered our courtyard, we saw that the soldiers had picked all the grapes from our vineyard, had put them in a big tub, which my mother used for boiling the laundry, and they were squashing them with their feet, while pouring pure alcoholic extract on that liquid and drinking the resulted mix.

But let's go back to the story with the priest....When the Russians came into the village and saw the priest - an old man, with a long white beard, a byzantine saint face -, they wanted to kill him. They dragged him next to a barn behind our house and, but the moment they were about to open fire on him, a man showed up out of nowhere, a man whose life-story is still a mystery to me. The priest knew him, but he did not tell anybody his story. So, this man spoke to the Russians, in Russian of course, and he saved the priest's life. As gratitude, the priest offered him a small house to live in and, as long as he had lived, he fed him and provided him with everything he needed. The man's name was Uray Iuliu. I think he was Polish-Hungarian. He knew all Slavic languages. He could also speak Italian, French and German. He set his mind to teach me these languages. He used to say that a language is learned through poetry, therefore, the first poem that I learned from him was Horatio, in Napolitaine dialect. I can still remember the words. But, after some thinking, he said that we had not started very well, and he decided that it would have been more suitable for me to start learning French. After a while, he told me that it would have been even better to combine language studies with getting to know the world, and so, we started making insectaria. His house was terrible. All the walls were covered with insects.

C.S.: *Did you ever use any of his characteristics to create one of your novels' characters?*

A.B.: Only a few, although I am obsessed with him. I do not know how to fully understand and explain him. I had finished high-school and I would still see him. He would come late at night, around midnight - in the countryside we always go to bed very early - to teach me the map of the sky. My poor mother was scared to death, thinking it was the *Securitate* knocking at our door.

After the priest had died, Uray would come daily to eat with us, so my instruction became even more systematic. Sometimes Uray would disappear and we would not know where he had gone. Many years later, when I became a teacher in a mountain village, in Valea Neagra, I ran into Uray there selling Bibles and glasses. He would keep looking for me to resume our French lessons, as if nothing had happened.

C.S.: *Where did you go to school?*

A.B.: I did the first four grades in the village school, in Berinta, then I went to school in the neighbouring village, in Copalnic-Manastur, because seven-grade teaching was cancelled. At the beginning, my mother did not want to let me go to school anymore. She was afraid because the distance was too big and the entire area was filled with wolfs. I had to cross a hill, through a forest. She told me to wait for a while, to grow older. And my father was saying that I would make a good farmer. Because they were afraid of the priest's patients, they kept me locked in the house, so I simply ran out the window to go to school, when they were away at work. What could have my mother done, the poor thing? She would accompany me with a lantern until we would reach the top of the hill, and then she would follow me with her eyes until I would enter the next village. I remember that once me and my mother were surrounded by a flock of wild pigs. It was winter, it was night, and it was terribly cold. We did not move, we were scared to death. They encircled us and then they left. Afterwards, my mother decided to send me to another village to live at an aunt's. I did not stay there for long either, because I was also taking care of my aunt's children and helping her husband with the farm chores, so I did not have much time left for studying. Finally, I moved to the school's boarding where I stayed for one year. In 7th grade I moved to Baia Mare. My father was working at the "Phoenix" factory. I was commuting everyday 25 km. It was very tiring for me, so I was transferred to the boarding school "Gheorghe Sincai". After a while, my mother concluded that I was not properly educated, and therefore, she sent me to live with an old lady, Ms. Puscasu, a former co-proprietor of the gold mines. Because her husband was in a labour camp, Ms. Puscasu had not left the house between 1948 and 1956. She used to live like the old lady in *Great Expectations*, but, in order to survive, she would rent out rooms to school children. She would take special care of us. Our day would begin with reading a paragraph from *The Code of Etiquette*. Then she would teach us how to sit properly at the table, with two books under our arms and one on our heads, or how to behave around a lady, to always stand up when a lady would enter a room. Therefore, if she entered the room a hundred times, we would have to stand up a hundred times. It was a pretty tiring ceremony for us children.

C.S.: *You were not alone there.*

A.B.: No. There were another two children renting rooms there. And one of them was the son of the village priest, the nephew of the priest I told you about, the one who was doing miracles. I left Ms. Puscasu, but after a few years, my mother sent me back there to "recivilise" me.

My mother played a tremendously important role in my life. After I finished high-school, we had a talk about what I should become. We had very different opinions on this. I was interested in the fine arts, and I dreamed of becoming a sculptor. I had had painting classes in school, and I also used to draw with Uray, who was not a brilliant drawer, but who knew what to tell me to make me draw better. So, under his guidance, I used to draw insects and landscapes. But what I felt truly passionate about was sculpture. We were living in a clayey area and, as my chore from spring till autumn was to mind the cows, I used to watch the animals and also work with clay all day long. I had hundreds of modellings. Human figurines.

C.S.: *You ended up modelling words.*

A.B.: Yes, sculpture was not meant to be either. The painting school in Baia Mare was cancelled, I did not have any money to pay for private lessons, and my mother thought that this kind of job was completely frivolous. My father had his mind made up as well. He would have liked to see me become a priest, but a farmer was not bad either! Anyways, he did not interfere too much, and let me decide for myself. Whereas for my mother, she had this fixed idea of me becoming a doctor. But not any kind of doctor, a veterinarian.

C.S.: *Why?*

A.B.: Why? Because the old village priest, Ghetie, had a son who was a famous teacher of comparative anatomy at the Veterinary Medicine Department of the Medical School in Bucharest, and he had told my mother to send me to him because he would have made a man out of me. And of course, my mother had been talked into believing that my future was in veterinary medicine. It was very difficult to contradict her, therefore I gave up, I went to Bucharest and I went to .... the Philosophy Department. I did not tell her because she did not know what I was studying anyways. Her only worry was to see me studying. She would bring me the lantern in the evening and she would let me read the whole night. I did not study anything for medical school. One of the reasons was that I did not have a book of anatomy, and anatomy was the subject of the admission exams. So I studied philosophy. I actually wanted to go to the Literature Department, which still existed in Bucharest at that time, but I had no idea what the conditions and the requirements were, I did not know were to go and who to talk to. When I went to Bucharest to take the admission exams it was my first time out of Baia Mare. I was very proud of myself that I managed without anybody's help, and especially without the professor's help who, although a famous scientist, I disliked falsely thinking that he was interfering with my life too much. For as long as I stayed in Bucharest I did not even go to see him. He came that autumn to hunt in Maramures because he also was a great hunter. And then that my mother found out the whole story, asking him: "How does my boy get along with everything?" "Which boy? He did not come to see me, I would have taken care of him to pass all the admission exams." My mother got really mad because I had not listened to her, and so she cut me off.

C.S.: *So this is how you finished with philosophy?*

A.B.: Yes, I made it on my own for three months. It was a nightmare. I did not and I will never forget those months. I ended up subsisting by doing various tricks. I used to sleep in a closet at the Institute for Oil and Gas, on Frumoasa Street. Once I discovered a stack of empty bottles and I sold them all for 30 *bani* a piece. Then I found a siamese cat and I sold it at the USSR Embassy for 300 lei. And of course, I spent them all immediately. And then, I do not remember how but I ended up sleeping with a friend of mine in the house of a composer, Ion Vasilescu, who was out of town. The man had a refrigerator for sale and we managed to sell it for more than the price which he had set on it, so we had money for some time. But the funds drained slowly. For a while, I pulled through by tasting foods in the capital's markets and sleeping in the Botanical Garden. I used to go to the market and ask: "And what's the price of the sour cream?" "This." I would taste it and say that "no, it's bad". "Have another taste, you'll see, it's not bad!" And so on. Then we decided that we could have started stealing. Both of us. We did not end up stealing, but we used to tell one another that that was the only solution. I remember that we used to wander around the Central Station, where we could have slept in the waiting area. I recall being with this friend of mine when we saw a man who was sleeping on a bench. He had two loafs of bread, some salami and canned food. We sat beside him, next to each other, thinking of stealing the man's food, and we even managed to do it but I suddenly felt sick, disgusted with myself, and I decided to go back home and listen to my commander-in-chief, my mother.

C.S.: *You simply made up your mind right there on the spot?*

A.B.: Yes.

C.S.: *And how did you manage to get home? How did you find the money for the train fare?*

A.B.: I did not have any money for the train ticket. It is a big distance from Bucharest to Baia Mare, so some soldiers taught me how to travel on top of the train without getting caught. They told me all the little details I needed to know to make it, how to sit on top of the train, how to be careful when we would pass through tunnels, because we had to pass through many tunnels, how to lock myself in the toilet, and what story to tell the ticket collector if he had found me. I have to tell you that their lesson served me well. I travelled all the way to Saratel, near Dej, without getting caught. However, I had been totally uninspired because I had got on a train that needed almost 24 hours to reach Baia Mare. I had actually got on the first train that was living, I wanted to get home as fast as possible. Once I had decided I had to live, I did not care anymore whether I was going to starve on the train or in Bucharest. We reached Saratel in the morning. There had been a landslide and the train was going very slowly. I had not eaten anything in hours, so I left my suitcase with some soldiers to look after it and I jumped down from the train to gather some darn dried out plums from the trees along the railway. While I filled my pockets with plums, the train had already gone but I caught up with it in the next station and, feeling cheerful that I had something to eat, I sat down on top of one of the cars with my legs hanging. I did not realise that from inside the car one might see my legs out of the window. And there they came after me, two inspectors, one at each end of the car, blocking my escape ways. A few times before, I had even jumped from one car to the next, I could have cared less about my life and the train and everything else.

C.S.: *So, at Saratel the ticket inspectors caught you.*

A.B.: Yes. They caught me and I started reciting to them the speech I had learned from the soldiers: "I am the son of a traffic controller from Baia Mare, I am a student at the school for traffic controllers...."

C.S.: *Why did you have to tell them that you were a student at the school for traffic controllers?*

A.B.: Because at that school they keep one's I.D., and thus, the inspectors could not ask me for any document to prove my identity. So: "My father is a traffic controller, he is going to pay you, I missed my parents...." and so on. They were very nice to me, they fed me, I believe I had never in my life eaten that well...

C.S.: *I bet you didn't, you were starving!*

A.B.: Then they put me in a first-class car....

C.S.: *If you had only known, you would have let yourself get caught from the start!*

A.B.: That's true! But how could I have known? Anyways, one station before reaching Baia Mare, I jumped down from the train, I clung to the last car, the post car, and the soldier who I had an understanding with waited for me in Baia Mare with my suitcase. This is how I got back home. Of course, I could not have stayed at home. There was no discussion about it. Stupidity has a price. "You go somewhere you can work and study for medical school", my mother decided. This is how all my troubles began and how I ended up with having so many different jobs.

C.S.: *What other jobs did you have? I knew you were a psychiatrist. I found out talking to you that you were also a teacher.*

A.B.: Oh, this happened later. At first, I found a job as an office worker at the Regional Office for Statistics. I got it with help from Ms. Puscasu - my mother's favourite person. My mother believed that Ms. Puscasu could have controlled and mastered me one way or the other. My boss used to rent a room at Ms. Puscasu's, and this is how I got the my first job. I used to work at the "Goods Management" department. It was crazy. One had to make these endless calculus and estimations, from which it had to derive that within the domestic trade there were more goods than in reality. My direct boss had, in his turn, more bosses, and so he placed me in the care of one of them who concluded that I was a disaster, that I had not the slightest inclination to being an office worker, that I had no "patience", a word that used to torture me at that time. He used to give me an assignment and, if I had not done it right, he used to tell me: "You don't have any patience, mister!"

C.S.: *With your lack of "patience", I gather you did not stay there for long.*

A.B.: True. They sent me to do an inventory at a collective farm in some village and, because I lacked even the necessary elementary knowledge, I determined that the administrator was at a huge loss, more than the value of the entire household, of the land around it and even of that part of the village together. Therefore, they fired me. They actually did not fire me, but my boss promoted me and made me responsible of the Foods Market in Baia Mare. What was going on there was unbelievable. I had to estimate the quantities of the products found in the market, how many eggs, how much bacon, sour cream, potatoes and other products were there. I had to take care of the scales as well. I did my work conscientiously for a while, until I learned the numbers. In fact, the peasants would come with the merchandise and then sell it. It did not matter. Then I learned the approximate numbers. So, I would just roughly decrease and increase those numbers according to how many people I thought there were in the market. I also learned the numbers from the socialist shops, and I would make my calculation so that the figures from the socialist shops were always higher than those from the individual farms. Therefore, once I went to the cinema and my boss caught me there. And this time I was obviously fired. However, I really wanted to get fired because I had to go every day to the market with Ms. Puscasu, who finally decided to get out of the house and, being a "market leader", I had to accompany her shopping. The most painful part of it all was the way back home from the market. I did not know how to walk with a lady on my arm and I did not know how to use the umbrella either. "Two steps, umbrella down, two steps, umbrella down!" We never synchronised our steps, which was terrible. And besides, I had many friends who were making fun of me whenever they saw me with the "old hag on my arm". There also was the bargaining part. And it was a bargaining for five *bani*, which were nothing to me but meant everything to her. And there was something else still. The atmosphere in Ms. Puscasu's house was really bad. She had a girl, who was a cashier at a cinema now, but who, when she was a young lady, fell in love with an Austrian football player. At that time they owned the gold mine and were reach. But the football player had not come to take her with him after everything that happened in our country, and she became an embittered spinster. As beautiful as she was, as embittered she became. She used to nag us all the time. So I decided that I had to leave, to leave the job, to leave the lodge and become independent. I thought that there was nothing left for me to do there.

C.S.: *Did you go back home?*

A.B.: Home? No way. I got a job at Sasar as an unskilled worker in the mine. I was working as a shotfirer assistant. It was a brutifying job. My entire existence was made up of mine, tavern, sleep; tavern, sleep, mine. I did not see any possibility for me to go to college, the old and persistent obsession of my mother and.... mine. In the mean time, it became my obsession as well. Any horizon had been closed down for me. The only thing left was death. It was then that I saw all the faces of death. I thought: there is nothing good coming out of me, there is nothing good coming out of what I have planned, so maybe it would be better to just ended it with life. Therefore, one day I remained longer by the wick. It was terrible. I was staying there by the dynamite that was about to go off. It was a long, long second, and I could see myself over and over again with a stupendous lucidity. Everything was clear extremely clear. And then, suddenly, I gave myself another chance. I ran. But I did not know if it were already too late. I woke up after the explosion. But I still did not know if it were too late. I could hear people shouting "Fire!", and I could not understand who and what was burning. But it was not me!

I left the mine. But again, it was out of the question to stay at home. So, I was an office worker at the registry office for a while. Then I was a forest worker, but I could not cope with it. It meant doing massive work, above my physical capacities. Therefore, I found another job as a substitute teacher in a village, Valea Neagra. It was close to Baia Mare but spiritually it was so far away that it seemed to be at the end of the world. The entire winter, I survived eating potatoes. The waters would destroy the bridges, blocking the road leading to

Baia Mare, and so we would basically be isolated there. It was a strange village, really strange. There was this teacher, who was a seventh-grade school graduate. It was the start of the collectivisation, and we had to go and convince the peasants to sign up for the collective farms. Actually, there was not much land to collectivise, and people's life was brutifying. They would work the whole week up in the mountains and when they would get their paychecks, they would come down to Selevetchi's tavern and drink everything inside. In autumn, people would sleep in shacks to guard their corn from the bears. And there was this thick darkness overlaying the entire village. We would only see the sun for a couple of hours a day. It was a nightmare.

C.S.: *How long did you stay there, in that village?*

A.B.: I stayed there almost a year. I used to sleep in the school building on a sack of leaves because, with only 375 lei per month, one could not do much. But because I had not written home for a long time, my mother came to see me. This time she took me home with her. And from that moment on, I started studying like crazy for the admission exams for college. I did not make it at the Veterinary Medicine Department, as my mother wished for, but she was happy anyway, knowing that I managed to get into medical school!

C.S.: *How did you, a medical school graduate, end up writing literature? As I understood from some notes, Mircea Zaciu played quite an important role.*

A.B.: That's true. Zaciu played an important role. I ended up writing literature in a rather unexpected way. My colleagues in medical school were very good students, extraordinary actually. In my group, there were students who would get only 9 and 10 grades, considering the fact that 5 and 6 were regarded as good grades in certain subjects where we had teachers from Cluj's old medical school. What I mean is that the teachers would make the difference between a 5 and a 10 by asking only one question. I remember that in microbiology the teacher once told me: "You have 8,75. I have to ask you another question." And I said: "Just give me 8." "I can't do that, what am I to do with the other 0.75?"

C.S.: *Anyway, how did you end up writing literature?*

A.B.: The year I got into college, a series of events took place that were to decide my future. That summer, I had a facial paresis, right before my summer exams, and therefore, I could not take them. In autumn, I also had a severe form of hepatitis, and so it was decided that I had to repeat the first year.

C.S.: *It seems that bad luck followed you. The rule was that who had to repeat the first year was expelled.*

A.B.: Exactly! The professor assigned to my case while I ha been hospitalised intervened for me at the dean and the provost, but he was not successful. I had not failed the exams, I just had not taken them. I went all the way up to the Ministry of Education, to Ilie Murgulescu, who was minister at that time. Nothing was solved. I went to see Emil Bodnaras in order to have him approve my examination. I was talking about *examination*, they were talking about *re-examination*.

How could there be a *re-examination* when I had not taken the exams in the first place? Finally, thanks to one of Emil Bodnaras' counsellors, I returned to school with the papers approved as I wished for, but it was too late because I had already missed too much time, about three months of classes, and I especially missed the practical projects. In the end, I had to repeat the first year but without having to take the admission exams again.

That was my most cultural year. Because I had studied very well the previous year and I also had a 30 % exemption due to medical reasons, I hanged my exemption above my bed and I started going to the university's library and read literature to recover my lost years. I began toying with the idea that I could write. I did not write anything in that period but the idea just obsessed me.

I did not like medicine during the first three years but I kept hoping that in the following years, when we would pass to doing the practical work, I would find a specialisation that I would enjoy. However, I had something to gain: I was a student. And the idea that I could upset my parents again terrified me. I stayed in medical school but the thought of writing just would not leave me alone. So, I decided to finish with this obsession. I told myself that the best way to do it was to write a story that would turn out to be bad. I wrote the story *The Earth*, and I wrote it with anger. However, I wrote it as best as I could because I did not want to reproach myself with anything. Nevertheless, I wanted to make a fool out of myself, to finish it with literature once and for all and to start being serious about medicine. I went with that story to the literary circle held by Mircea Zaciu. I did not make a fool out of myself, as I had hoped for. Zaciu actually liked my story. He publish it in the magazine *Tribuna*.

C.S.: *So your debut wain* Tribuna*! What year was that?*

A.B.: It was in 1960. I think it was the same year and the same month as Ion Alexandru's debut. Those were tough years. One more time, I had some tough years. I had discovered literature but, at the same time, I had to study for medical school so that I would not lose my scholarship. But I also attended all the classes of Modern Literature, Universal Literature and Comparative Literature at the Philology Department in Cluj, all the Philosophy classes held by D.D. Rosca, and the History of Art classes at the Fine Arts Institute. I also wrote other short stories which were all gathered to make my first book, *The Cape of Good Hope*, with a foreword signed by Zaciu. It is not such a good book. Nevertheless, it has a merit: the subjects of those stories were the germs of my later novels. The atmosphere and the obsessions of that time haunted me my entire life. That first book had another significance as well: it was my editorial debut and later, it turned out to play quite an important role during the job repartition.

C.S.: *Did you also discover something that you liked in medicine?*

A.B.: Yes. In the forth year, I discovered psychiatry. I have to tell you that my teacher said that I had it in me to become a psychiatrist. Therefore, I became a member of the psychiatry club and I also had to read tones of additional books. I could go to the clinic any time I wanted to because I had permanent access there. Zaciu, on the other hand, gave me the books which he considered to be absolutely necessary for me to keep abreast of true values. I tried my best to reconcile the two but I had started to lean more and more towards psychiatry.

C.S.: *You had to choose again.*

A.B.: Yes, a real tragedy. But neither this time was I the one who actually chose. You know, I have always wanted to be myself, to be independent, and yet there were always others taking the decisions for me. Destiny or something else, I do not know how to call it, turned my plans upside down. That is, those plans which did not match its plans. At that time, I had the impression that things were going the wrong way, but now, looking back, I realise that they were exactly the things that were supposed to happen to me.

I finished medical school with a good average. My final thesis was *Shakespeare in psychiatry.* Now the paper looks completely outdated and foolish but, at that time, it meant a lot. I think that in Romania there had not been papers written yet on psycho-pathology in literature. Those attempts were of great help to me later because I had read everything that one could read on Shakespeare in our country at that time. And then came the day when I had to defend my thesis. Well, I have to tell you that there was a teacher who haunted me my entire life, the Scientific Socialism teacher. In my first year, he did not let me take the exam. He told me to settle my things with the dean's office. What I had to settle with the dean's office I did not know. At the dean's office, I had been told that maybe there was something out of order with my file at cadres. At cadres, they stared at me: "Go see the teacher to tell you exactly what is this all about." And then I found out that they wanted to expel me.

C.S.: *Why?*

A.B.: At that time, my father was very ill, he had been intoxicated with lead. And he would only go to see a doctor if I had come with him. Therefore, when my mother called and told me "Come home to go with your father to the doctor!", I went immediately home. When I got there, I found my father on the porch, who said to me: "Leave me alone and go look after the cow." I went to the barn and I saw that the cow had an allergic reaction, it had vesicles on the respiratory passages. In the countryside, people call this disease "terrible frog" because it makes the animals die due to respiratory failure. Since I was a child I knew that, in these situations, you just had to stick your hand on the animal's throat and break the vesicles so that it could breathe. I did all these and then I went and called a friend who was a vet in the neighbouring village, about 20 km away. While I was on the phone with him, I heard a voice who told me: "Hey, you there, who are you? What business do you have to talk about with the son of a kulak?". And I answered back: "Leave me alone, mister!". I was so agitated, afraid that the cow could die, that.... I swore at him. In the evening, we ended up with a policeman at our door, who announced me that I was "invited" at the city hall by the first secretary of the Lapus district, the district we were part of. "Leave me alone, mister", I said, "I don't care about the first secretary. It's not him that I came home for." And the policeman: "You can't say no, because I have orders to bring you in even if I have to tie you up." Then my father said: "Let's go, I'm coming too." How could I have let my ill father get out of the house? I went alone, accompanied by the policeman. At the city hall, a real presidium. It was already night by the time we got there, and there were gas lamps on the tables. The policeman went inside with me. And I said: "Good evening." Nobody answered. And then this guy stepped forward and swore at me: "You, you have the courage to defy me.... .....!" And I said: "Sir, I do not know who you are, I do not know what you want, but you started talking to me on the phone while I was having a conversation with someone. It is not right. It is not legal. However, if I did something wrong, I apologise, it was an emergency." I did not feel the danger at all. But he kept pushing me into the wall. And then I realised that he had been drinking. A lot. He stepped on my foot. And then I put my hand in his neck and I told him: "If you lay your hands on me, I'll beat you to death!". He went back and sat down at the table and started questioning me: "Who is your mother? Who is your father?". I said: "Leave me alone, sir, because they are asking me all these questions all the time at school.". I slammed the door and I left. This was the entire conversation.

Let's return now to Ratiu, the teacher I was telling you about. So, I went to the cadres. And there I found out that those people from my village had sent a letter to the dean's office, a letter in which they had "turned me in". The man at cadres told me: "Look hear, mister, the people from the district's cadres had sent a letter stating that you had criticised the party's politics.". "No, sir, the whole story was the cow, not politics. But I know for sure that I cannot prove it against everybody. However, there has to be at least one honest man from all those over there. And, if one person confirms my story, I hope you will believe me."

Who do you think told the truth? The policeman who took me there. He saved me from being expelled.

C.S.: *You were lucky.*

A.B.: Later, I ran into Ratiu again. I am leaping six years forward. The same Ratiu was now on the committee which was grading the thesis papers. I was really proud of having written a paper that was going to "blow them away". So, my paper reached the committee and the Pediatrics teacher, who was also the secretary of the committee, called me one night before the day I was supposed to defend my thesis, and told me: "Sir, what have you written in that paper? Be aware that Ratiu is going to throw you out!". "But what did he say?" "Well, he said that it was reactionary. Do something and defend it as best as possible!"

Then I went to see Ms. Aurelia Sarbu, the teacher who had supervised my paper and who had been taking care of me all those years, and I told her the whole story. "Your paper is good, he has nothing to reproach you with, but you cannot mess with this crazy guy."

I went again to see the Pediatrics teacher and I asked him: "Sir, please, would you just think of a phrase or two of what Ratiu said. I only have a few hours left and I have to counteract." And he remembered Ratiu saying that I had not judged the characters I analysed in my paper according to the respective social conditions. Then I recalled a phrase written by Marx on Shakespeare and Homer, in which he stated that one cannot judge the two of them according to the respective social conditions. I took Marx' book and skimmed through every page until I found that phrase, the phrase which actually saved my paper.

The next day, in front of the committee, I told Ratiu that confronting him with regard to Marxism themes was useless, because I did not know as much as he did anyway. But then I added that, however, when I wrote my paper, and I was looking him straight in the eye, I had in mind a phrase Marx wrote, "you remember", I said, "from that page, where he states that, as regards Homer and Shakespeare, one cannot judge the two of them according to the social conditions and therefore, I structured my paper in that way."

"Yes, yes!", he nodded, "but why didn't you write this in your paper?". He lowered my grade with one point, but at least I managed to save my thesis paper.

C.S.: *And then the repartition came.*

A.B.: Exactly. My teacher told me that there were two vacancies in the psychiatry field and that she would see to get me to her department, no matter where I would be sent. She said that the only thing I had to do was to just accept a position somewhere in psychiatry. She was probably hoping that I would follow her at her lecturer's chair. I had read a lot about psychosis, I was particularly interested in schizophrenia and I would have liked to do research on the metabolism of lysergic acid and of mescaline. However, it would have been actually very difficult to do it because it was impossible to find those substances and to do serious research in Romania of that time. But again destiny, disguised in chance, decided differently. The vacancy in Siret was taken by a student who had an overall average higher than my 9 points. There was only one available psychiatry position left, in Zalau, which would have been extremely convenient to me, but a colleague, who had intended to apply to the Ministry of Internal Affairs, changed his mind on the way to the Repartition Committee. Thus, my psychiatry dream was pretty much over.

C.S.: *I don't understand. Didn't you have a specialisation in psychiatry?*

A.B.: Well, actually I didn't. I had finished general medicine. One gets the specialisation in about six years. So I had to look for something else.

C.S.: *As general doctor?*

A.B.: Yes. As a general doctor in Maramures. And again, by a strange accident, I would be a doctor in the same village I had previously been a teacher, in Firiza, in Valea Neagra village. But I had swore to myself that I would have never set foot again in Valea Neagra. Therefore, I did not take that job over and I stayed in Cluj. Here, my debut book turned out to be of great help to me. I got a job as typist at the Writers' Union because I had something published. I spent the following months, from October till the 1st of April of next year, sleeping on a door which I would position on the table. They used to have some very nice, upholstered doors at the Writers' Union. So, every night, I would put one of the doors on the table, and I would sleep covered with the country's and party's flags. The only problem was that in the morning my back hurt dreadfully. As long as I was not hired as an editor, there were practically no chances for me to get a house, and finding a place on my own with the wage I had at that time was practically impossible. There were vacancies, and there were promises for me, but they were just promises, nothing more. Once, when the back pain was so bad that I could not take it anymore, I got up and, angry as I was, I wrote a memo to the region's first secretary, Maxim Berghianu. It seems that he read my memo because, one night, I heard someone knocking at my door. I was up on the table and I did not even have the time to get up and see who it was, when "a citizen" just walked in the room. "Are you Comrade Buzura? Please, don't let me disturb you!", he said to me while I was trying to jump off the table. The next day, I was told by the editor-in-chief, Dumitru Mircea, that I was going to get a job at the magazine *Tribuna*. And they even gave me a house.

C.S.: *What position were you hired on?*

A.B.: Editor of the scientific section. They used to have a page dedicated to scientific matters. And science was a passion of mine. Actually, I was in charge of both the scientific and the foreign literature pages. And I believe that I did some good work while I was there. Today, when I look through the collection of magazines I have, I am not ashamed of what I had done in those years. I think I automatically changed the magazine's perspective, as I was always looking for what was new and I was also trying to move towards a philosophy of science.

C.S.: *When was this?*

A.B.: I was hired at *Tribuna*, symbolically I would say, on 1 April 1965. And it has been 1st of April ever since!

C.S.: *You finally found your peace of mind. In 1966, your second book of short stories was published,* Why does the eagle fly.

A.B.: Well, there's a story behind that book as well. So, when I got hired, I realised that medicine was getting further and further away from me. I was well informed about everything that came out in psychiatric literature, but I could not do research anymore, that is, not successfully. And it was not truly my dream to become a treatment doctor, who would first speak and then write recipes. Actually, I could not picture myself seeing thirty patients per day, that was not what I was interested in. I kept on writing. I was not satisfied with my first book but the experience had been useful to me. I had understood which were my weaknesses but I had also realised that I had a capacity to write. However, I used to read immensely. I had an awful hunger for literature, a fear which urged me to catch up with my generation. I had realised how much time I had lost and I did not know what to do to win it back. And in this context, medicine proved to be very helpful, because it disciplined me to be very serious about achieving complete knowledge of the field I was dealing with. Namely, when I was writing, I had to have the feeling that I was doing scientific research, all the terminology had to be exact, the conclusion had to be the necessary conclusion that would logically result from the given data. Writing seemed too complicated for the culture I had back then.

C.S.: *Were you thinking about writing a novel? Three or four years had already passed between you debut book and the second one.*

A.B.: Exactly. I kept my writing rhythm, and I still publish a book every three or four years.

C.S.: *How did you get the idea of writing* The Absentees*?*

A.B.: I'd had that idea for a long time. I've had all my novel ideas for a long time. However, there was something else about that novel. I had always considered myself unprepared for writing. I lived and I am still living with this obsession of the recovering. For me, it was both an inconvenience and a support. It helped me keep my mind awake, and always try to get to know things.

C.S.: *And today, are you still unsatisfied?*

A.B.: No. I am terribly unsatisfied. I constantly have this strange state of mind, which I do not exactly know how to define, a state of eternal debut. At that time, I was not aware of what literature meant, but today, when I am.... I do not have any excuse.

C.S.: *At the beginning, did you believe that the two published books were representing you?*

A.B.: No, they were just a formality for me to enter the world. They expressed some good things but I was far from being satisfied with them. This dissatisfaction prompted me to write literature.

C.S.: *Are you a slow writer?*

A.B.: I wrote the first volumes really easily. Now I became a very slow writer.

C.S.: *When you are writing, do you need to have a certain ambience? A certain place to write in? A certain time?*

A.B.: During college, I used to write easily at night, after my roommates went to bed. At home, I used to write all night long by lamp light, while my family was sleeping. Then I got used to writing only at night.

C.S.: *And what about daytime?*

A.B.: I would look through what I wrote at night.

C.S.: *Returning to* The Absentees, *how did you write the novel?*

A.B.: It was some time around 1967. I felt that I did not do my best with the first two books and I set my mind to try again. If it had not work out fine, I think I would have had the strength to give up literature. I wrote *The Absentees* but, for many reasons, I hesitated to give it to print. First, it seemed to me that I wrote it too easily. Second, I was aware of the fact that it did not turn out exactly the way I would have wanted it to. Third, I was afraid of a failure, because the novel was pretty different, pretty new I might say, compared to everything else that was being written in Romania at that time.

C.S.: *After the novel came out, some reviews stated that* The Absentees *marked the moment that Romanian literature finally synchronised with Western literature. Maybe your page dedicated to foreign literature in* Tribuna *might have proved useful to you in this context. Other critics wrote that the novel was a re-connection to tradition. Did you have any models?*

A.B.: No. I mean, I had an intellectual model, a model of how to work, which was very dear to me: Rebreanu. I liked the idea of intellectual work. I liked seriousness. Rebreanu had rigorous seriousness and moral responsibility in his every gesture. I liked of course many other writers for various reasons. I believe that Shakespeare, whose work I know very well, is the embodiment of absolute perfection.

I have to make a confession. With regard to my first two books, the critics made references to writers who I had not even read at that time. As I told you before, I was really behind with my readings. To me, being abreast of literature meant taking up literature from the very beginning and read it page by page. This is another legacy science left me with. One has to know everything that has happened before in that specific field of one's interest. Thus, I had a feeling of dissatisfaction: so many unread books, so many events for which I could not find a place in my mental formula, although I knew that they were suitable for literature. This feeling of the recovering haunted me my entire life. So, after I had written *The Absentees*, I was afraid to take it to print. I kept postponing it. I thoroughly read it over and over again. I kept waiting, I don't know for what exactly. Until one day when I plucked up enough courage to go and leave it at Dacia Publishing House. It came out really soon, with only a few unimportant changes, which were probably done according to the editor's personal taste.

C.S.: *Who was the book editor?*

A.B.: Viorica Marii, D.R.Popescu's sister. The book was out but I did not trigger in me that feeling I had been waiting for, the feeling of liberation, of well-being, quite on the contrary, I felt a certain anxiety. And the truth is that the novel had an odd existence. After it was published, there was a review signed by Dan Laurentiu, in which he stated that the novel was successful. It was a surprise because, well, I did not expect such a reaction.

C.S.: *The critics' response came as a big surprise to you.*

A.B.: A total surprise, which swept me off my feet, as it is said.

C.S.: *The entire elite of the Romanian critics wrote about your novel.*

A.B.: Yes, it was amazing. At that time, I was obsessed with one critic in particular, the only one who had truly believed in me ever since the time of my first book of short-stories. His name was Valeriu Cristea. He used to work at the magazine *Romania literara* and he made comments on every short-story I had published. And honestly, I was mostly afraid of his reaction. Thus, I did not expect such a warm welcome from the critics, I rather anticipated the usual polite critics, black-and-white or even grey.

In addition, I had the feeling that my writing was "something else". As I told you before, I had not seen before this way of writing and thinking in Romania. I had also written the novel very easily, and I even was intimidated by my inner confrontation. I had risked tremendously and I had an awful fear of failure. All this made me look forward, with anxiety, to the reactions the novel would awaken. And then, there was this round table which acclaimed it and which surprised me a lot.

However, the book had an unusual fate. I had received the Writers' Union Award for it, I was also awarded with the "Cultural Merit", and then my novel was banned, following the theses of July 1971. There was a long list which was never published, and *The Absentees* too was on that list.

In 1971, when the book was banned, nobody was writing anything about my work, I was in very low spirits, my wings had been cut off and I did not even know why. I think that that was the moment when I started better understanding the world. The incident with *The Absentees* was a necessary evil, which made me focus on the political and social mechanisms. I tried to object to the novel's banning and thus, I went to Zaharia Stancu, to the Central Party Committee, I went everywhere. I remember that, after a few months, due to one of my protesting visits, I found the book on display in a bookshop window in Bucharest. It was evidence that the ban had been removed. However, the books were not being sold to anyone, not even to me. Today, I do not even have a single copy of *The Absentees*. Anyways, at that time, the novel received quite a lot of attention from the Western press because it was a banned novel. Many books were slowly put back in circulation, but *The Absentees* remained on the list of banned titles. And of course there is this question mark still hanging over the book. Last year, another memo emerged. I had not seen it, but a few libraries called me up to tell me that the novel was withdrawn again. First, I checked on my own by going to various libraries and the title was indeed not on their listings. Then I asked Nicolae Manolescu - who had already let me know about this new banning - to check at the Academy Library and at the University Library in Bucharest. It was not there either. The new list with banned titles was issued, as far as I could find out, as a consequence of the re-examination of the 1971 list. What is strange is that the novel was referred to even after its withdrawal from the libraries.

C.S.: *How many copies were published?*

A.B.: I think there were somewhere between fifteen and thirty thousand copies.

C.S.: *Are there any similarities between your own background and the character of Mihai Bogdan? He is a psychiatrist.*

A.B.: He is a psychiatrist because I wanted to be on familiar grounds. And then I felt like I was practising my occupation by writing about psychiatry. It still hurt that I had to give up psychiatry and, in that way, I felt that I was not entirely betraying it.

C.S.: *Do you find the critics' input helpful? Do you care about what they say about your work?*

A.B.: I cared about that my entire life. How to say it.... Well, I have to explain something. I care about the opinion of some of them, of those who have talent, good taste and are honest. Not everybody who writes prose is a true writer. Literature has a tremendous power to attract ambitious, untalented opportunists. The books are, for many, just a pretext to climb up in various administrative or political hierarchies. Empty cans make the loudest noise, right? Without the support of real critics, it would have been difficult to assert the books and the ideas that were worthwhile promoting. We stand on a barricade that needs to be defended in order to truly have a full-scale existence. It is obvious that they, the critics, cannot make a writer better or worse than he/she actually is. *The Absentees* was my exam, my confrontation with myself, and I said to myself that, for the time being, I had passed it. Anyway, it was my hardest challenge, which irrevocably convinced me to continue with literature.

C.S.: *One of the critics commented once on the symbol-images* *in your novel. He made a reference to that man who was walking in mud against the current.*

A.B.: I never thought about it.

C.S.: *Not even when you wrote about that room with the locked doors?*

A.B.: Yes, in that case, yes. That is an aforethought image. *The Absentees* was intended to be a metaphor for loneliness and despair. A futile cry. Actually, a futile revolt.

C.S.: *Of all the books you have ever written, which one is the dearest to you?*

A.B.: The one I am going to write next!

C.S.: *Does this mean that, after you wrote and published a book, you are not interested in its destiny anymore?*

A.B.: No, absolutely not. Every time I start writing a book, I set a goal for myself, a personal performance that I need to achieve, and which I care a lot about. Once the book is finished, I am only interested in the taking the next step.

C.S.: *I was in some way surprised to read somewhere that you wrote* The Voices of the Night *for its last phrase, that you had built the novel starting from that particular phrase, which you'd had in your mind from the very beginning.*

A.B.: We have to go all the way back to *The Faces of Silence* so you could understand the mental mechanisms which I am building my novels with. As I have said before, with each novel I decide on a task for myself. For instance, it would have been very easy for me to write about peasants, but I have always rejected this theme and I passed on to something else, which seemed to be beyond my abilities. I moved to a different environment, to a different psychology, to a different typology. And I did this only because thus, I had forced myself to get to know more, to understand more, to try more, to walk on a path on which I had never walked before.

I told you already about that priest, Ghetie. *The Faces of Silence* is based on a certain event, on an enigma of that time. I said before that Ghetie the priest had taken care of my teacher, Uray. But he had taken care of someone else as well, a man who was hiding in the priest's house and would only come out at night. Just a few neighbours knew about the priest's guest. They knew that he was a partisan, one who tried to challenge the system which was just starting to develop. And then I found out that he was not the only one in the area. One day, the priest's guest disappeared as suddenly as he had appeared. I heard that he might have been murdered. I do not even know his name. But his face has been imprinted in my mind so well that I could draw it.

C.S.: *Don't you think it would be interesting for the reader to find out how you created your characters, how you managed to transform people from real life into novel characters?*

A.B.: I would probably bound the reader's imagination. However, I can picture my characters so well when I write that I could draw them. I can even see their hands. My entire life, I have had an obsession with hands. This is my starting point with a person. The hands. For instance, I once met a person, a strong man, well-built, who looked like a fighter. Well, his hands seemed to me very frail, very soft in comparison to the rest of his body. When I was a child, he used to stroke me on my head, but he did it in a clumsy way. I used to feel his clumsy caress and it annoyed me. My father, for example, never caressed me. And my mother, just a little. Very little. But my father never caressed me. My father's hands were rough, and very strong.

C.S.: *Let's go back to the priest's guest.*

A.B.: Yes, so I later found out that he was a partisan who was hiding and that he later died. There were many people hiding in the neighbouring villages too, people who ran away from the collectivisation and were resisting the system in their own way.

I remember that one day I was taking care of some cows in the next village, Copalnic, when I heard gunshots coming from the forest. I was used to hearing gunshots, there had been many of those there in the forest. For many years after the war, one could still find bullets in the area. Children would play with them, they would throw them in a fire and the bullets would explode. So, suddenly I heard continuous gunshots. I knew from other people's experience that, in such circumstances, one should duck to the ground, so I ducked. But I could not stay there for long because I was curious to see what was happening. I got up and ran to the road. I was a bit scared too. I did not care that much about me getting shot, I cared more about the cow. I knew it would have been very bad if they had shot my cow. I saw a car coming out of the forest, a jeep, many soldiers and a man being dragged by his legs from the forest and thrown into the car, like a sack of potatoes, without the slightest respect for death. Like an animal that has just been shot. And, on the contrary, in Maramures, people have extreme respect for the dead and for death in general. This is something that can be seen in the mortuary rituals. So, I have always expected some kind of respect from everybody, respect for death or for the unknown, something which I was used to.

C.S.: *Have you ever found out who that person was?*

A.B.: I tried. I kept asking here and there in order to discover who he was, but nobody knew. It was my first experience of that kind. And it had nothing to do with death. I was used to death. I was obsessed with the miners' funerals. They were held in the evening, accompanied by the miners' fanfare. I could often hear those songs, which made a strong impression on me. But that was my first contact with a person who got shot. I knew about the partisans, I sometimes heard their names whispered, but they were some kind of a legend, I knew that noone could have caught them. It was exactly like in the fairy tales. For instance, in Maramures, nobody thinks that Pintea had died, although everybody knows that he was shot "with three silver bullets". He haunts that region like a ghost. He is still very much alive. The same was true for the partisans. They were very much alive even though noone had their physical representation. They were legends. One could hear about their "courage deeds", that they caught I don't know what party activist and that they actually "shoed" him or that they made him eat his party membership card and all kinds of stories.

C.S.: *You still have not told me how the partisan in the village got to be a character in* The Faces of Silence.

A.B.: The man who got shot kept obsessing me, and so did the man who the village priest had protected and about who the people later said that got shot as well. The two images overlapped, I added other details, other incidents, other images of those who had fought in the Fagaras and Apuseni mountains. I followed their tracks and I was convinced that people had fought heroically for years. Every incident I came across, every tragedy I found out about would have been enough to make a novel. After the war, there were constant fights going on there.... When I went to Valea Neagra as substitute teacher, I found there another type of fighters in the mountains. They too belonged to the legend. And there were others, the ones who had opposed the Russians when they had occupied Sighet. It was said that, in Borsa, they had built cannons out of cherry trees with which they had intended to free Sighet.

C.S.: *Cannons made of cherry trees?*

A.B.: There were legends that were being created, while we were living them. Their image was super-hyperbolized by the ones who were telling the stories. At the same time, I had the very real imagine of those who were looking for the resistence members. And I especially knew the local bosses. For instance, there was Rusu, the man I told you about before, and who had frightened the entire area. There was another one, Aron, who ended up so bad, as if he had been cursed. He went mad. He started believing that there was gold in his cellar. He used to endlessly dig down there. During the day, he would just sit on his porch and, when the cars with the commuters would pass by, the workers would spit on him, would cover him in spit from head to toe, they were the people who had left the village because they were afraid of him.

A neighbour of mine, who is still alive today, had been in prison for a few years because of Aron, on the grounds that he had stood against the collectivisation. After he got out of prison, he had one obsession: to punish all those who had falsely testified against him at the trial out of fear. He had an entire list and he used to carry it with him everywhere he went. About three years ago, I ran into him for the last time. He showed me the list and told me: "See here, out of the whole list, this is the only one who is left and even he has cancer!"

C.S.: *They had all been punished by providence?*

A.B.: Yes, he wanted to punish them with his own hands but providence got ahead of him. However, he told me how he had wanted to punish this activist, Rusu. He used to ride his bike in the forest around the places that he knew Rusu used to go. He intended to find him alone and kill him. He always had his knife with him and he was just waiting for the right moment to come. He told me that, finally, he had run into Rusu and, the moment he had found himself in front of the guy, he had taken out the knife and he had said to him: "Hey you, you turned my life upside down, you destroyed me, you sent me to jail...." and so on. And he said that, when he had grabbed Rusu by the neck, the guy just peed on him. Literally. And then he asked me: "Man, how could one put a knife into a man who is peeing his pants?". He did not consider Rusu a valid adversary anymore, and so he let him go.

So, these were events that were becoming living legends right in front of my eyes. Hence, the atmosphere in *The Faces of Silence*. The novel was written based on the idea of trying to know those who had stood against something. To understand another aspect of the issue, the viewpoint of those who seemed defeated, and not only the viewpoint of those who considered themselves winners. I was actually interested in the perspective of the defeated, as compared to the winners' perspective, two different ways of perceiving history. And I wrote a three-hundred-page novel. It was not such a big deal. It was done mostly out of memories. I lad let myself be driven by memories, more by legend than by the clean-cut truth. I had always been haunted by those images. Anyways, I had an amazing luck. I have to tell you that, while I was writing, I had collected a huge amount of material.

C.S.: *How do you do your research?*

A.B.: I talk to people, I go to the places I am about to write....

C.S.: *And when you start writing, do you already have the image of the book, do you already know how it is going to come out?*

A.B.: Yes, I have a very clear image of it.

C.S.: *You stated in an interview that when the third and last book of the trilogy* The Death Wall *would be published, it would be very clear what you had intended to express. Doesn't it happen to you to change the initial project while you are writing?*

A.B.: Yes, it does, I do not distribute the material well. I wanted each of the three novels of the trilogy to be independent but I did not distribute their substance well enough. For instance, if I had wanted *Refuges* to be totally independent, I should have also included the chapter "Sabin", which actually appears in *The Way of the Ash*. In this way, the novel would have been complete and I would have left other doors open. As I said before, I have always talked about what others believe and say, but I have never said anything about what I, the author, believe about the world. And, if it happened that I disappeared, I would have only one regret: that I did not say what I believed about the world, not only as a writer but also as a journalist. With the complete severity and sincerity that the world we live in deserves. Literature is not enough.

C.S.: *You wrote somewhere that, if you were to live another 20 years and if you were to be healthy and if.... and if.... , then, considering the fact that you published a book every other three or four years, you could write another four, five volumes. A few years ago, you expressed a wish to write a short novel,* The Extras *(interesting title). Did you start working on it?*

A.B.: No, because in the meantime the title has been taken.

C.S.: *How so? Was it a coincidence?*

A.B.: I don't know anymore. But something similar happened to me with Laurentiu Fulga. I had published a fragment entitled "It Is Night and It Is Cold, Noblemen", and he later had a book with the same title published. Anyway, I had projects of short novels before, but I don't know what happens along the writing process, but, every time, they all came out long.

C.S.: *We digressed from the discussion we were having about* The Faces of Silence. *You said that you had collected a great amount of material.*

A.B.: Yes, it was huge. I had a massive factual data collection but it was not structured all that well. I had one conclusion which was clear and besides that, facts, more facts, and even more facts. But I felt that between the facts and the conclusion I had missed the people. I dealt with legend and politics, with the legends about those people and the politics of that time, which I felt bound to contest; but I missed the people, the characters. I had neglected the psychologies. And then, I discovered, or I convinced myself of another truth that regards the job of being a writer: in the end, the novel is character and structure. I had the structure, but I missed the characters. In the meantime, I had also realised that I had to start writing only when the characters having those features I bestowed them with could have actually lived, could have had a history of their own, could have found their way in the world, could have had a life. And from that moment onwards, every time I wrote a book, I waited until the characters were so alive and so real that they started bothering me. My house would become so filled with them, that I could not stand them anymore. This is how alive they were.

C.S.: *Why did you say you were lucky?*

A.B.: I had an absolutely amazing luck. I was travelling by train to Bucharest and, in the compartment, I happened to meet the man who had run the suppression against the partisans in the Apuseni mountains. That was my luck, which made me to completely change the structure of my book. Actually, I even threw away what I had written before. It seemed ridiculous to me. I started the book again from scratch but I had to follow the steps of those fighters, to talk to those who took part in the fights.

C.S.: *In the book, did you depict them the way they actually were when you met them?*

A.B.: No, I did not picture them like that, I combined the stories I had known from Maramures with what I had learned from the Apuseni or Fagaras mountains. I recreated the people. I took new details and events from those I had met, and the fact that I had actually got to known some of them in person made me feel confident of my work. I wrote it very easily. Actually, *The Faces of Silence* is the novel that I wrote the easiest although, I think, it is the longest of my novels. I do not remember the exact number of pages but I recall writing it as if I were in a state of trance. What did not come out right at the desk at night would be solved in my sleep. I think there were about six months in which I almost didn't get any sleep at all.

It was a special sleep and it also was.... within the novel's atmosphere. I had always pictured volumes II, III and IV in my mind but I have written them yet. I had gathered so many events and details that were enough to write another book. For instance, I was interested in continuing *The Faces of Silence* because I was obsessed with the fate of this Magureanu, regarding the disappearance of that type of peasant we had known by reading Rebreanu, regarding the tragedy of the disappearance of the last genuine peasant. I was interested in the process of transforming these people into lumpen-proletariat. I had decided to continue with a second volume, I even had everything put in order. However, every time I was about to start, after I would have systematically structured everything, just when I was on the verge of beginning writing, I would ask myself: "Wouldn't it be better to just leave it for later and concentrate on a different environment?" And this was equally obsessing.

C.S.: *And you started* Vanities*?*

A.B.: And I started *Vanities*. Because I kept saying to myself to leave aside the second volume of *The Faces of Silence* for later, for when I would not be able to travel around the country collecting data anymore, and for when I would be more experienced. Here is a topic which is there at my disposal, at any time. In our country, well, one can expect just about anything to happen. Not to be able to get out of the house or to travel out of your own town. Not to be allowed to do it. Knowing that if I ran out of topics, I still have one left is reassuring. Maybe it would have been an error to continue that story, I don't think it would have made me be passionate about the narrative and the psychologies. Everything was old inside me. I was interested in the idea of good performance. Performance towards myself and what I had wrote. Namely, I wanted to walk a new path which would have required all my energy. And this is how I ended up with writing *Vanities*.

In a way, *Vanities* is similar to *The Absentees*, but by accident, due to the environment. Otherwise, the structures are different. I was no longer interested in the life of professor Cristian, not entirely I mean, but I was rather interested in that time he spent in jail, I was interested in the deprivation of freedom, and I was especially attracted by a chapter which is missing from the published book, a very long chapter.

C.S.: *Why is it missing?*

A.B.: The censorship took it out. Life after confinement in prison. His friends distancing from him, the isolation, the time when he started asking himself where had he experienced true human solidarity, outside prison or rather inside.

C.S.: *The obsession with the Canal.*

A.B.: Yes, yes. I once met a man who enlightened me with regard to this subject. You know how it is, you meet someone who just enters your life in a strange way, and you cannot get rid of that person anymore, and when you finally manage to do it, you actually start looking for that person again. I talked to so many people who were sent to the Canal, people who suffered tremendously, but only this man that I ran into by pure chance, well, only this man managed to describe the life at the Canal that suggestively to me, to touch those sensitive parts inside me that would have made me research the issue further. In *Vanities*, I wrote about him and about his experience, and then I mentioned him again in *The Road of Ash*. He is the character named Socoleanu and I have a feeling that I am going to come back to him because he is not complete yet. The world that he uncovered to me is far more interesting than the world I managed to describe. And I think I will return to this character. He wanted to meet me because he had read my work and so we became friends. However, he had a great influence on me. He was a subtle psychologist and, with grace, he would point out to me many psychologic details that escaped my attention. For instance, this sort of things would always happen when we went go together to a restaurant. I have to tell you that he used to be a representative from the National Peasants Party. He had played an important part in history, but this is not what impressed me about him, but rather the way he would introduce me into his world. At that time he was a driver, but he had been a representative and a lawyer before, as well as a very good journalist during the Vienna Dictate. I have his memoirs which are first class. As I was saying, we used to go together to the restaurant and he would point someone out to me: "Look at that guy, the one over there and the other one there. All three of them had done time in prison". I was amazed, there had passed 15 years since the last political prisoners were freed, and I would ask him:

"But have you met them?". "Oh, no, no, no", he would tell me, "but there are some gestures that betray one who has done time before. See how they are eating, how they dash upon the food?". "See how they are protecting their food? Look at the way he is holding his hands! Look, we can ask them if you want." And he would get up, would go to that man and would directly ask him: "Where were you, in which prison?". The man would be so surprised. However, he had a very pleasant and friendly way of behaving and so, the other man would not react violently. He was a man full of charisma. And this is how he had won my sympathy, with all these small details. If he had told me only a great quantity of facts, I believe I would not have cared about him that much.

Sometimes he would come to my office at the magazine with a bag full of onions, carrots and potatoes. He had a pension of about 400 *lei*, but he never let me pay for his coffee, he could not stand any kind of humilities. I would let him pay for his meal as well, not to upset him in any way. So, he would come to my office, but because we could not talk there due to all the fuss and agitation around us, we would go to a coffee-shop. If I wanted to buy cigarettes, he would tell me to go with him to a certain kiosk down town. And, while I was ordering my pack of cigarettes, he would stand by the entrance, with his hands at his back and he would just stare at the salesman, who would start sweating. I would get my cigarettes and we would leave and he would suddenly become fully satisfied with himself. I had not realised, not the first time, nor the second or the third, why he wanted me to get my cigarettes from that specific place. Finally, when I had a chance to look at both of them, I realised that there was something going on with those two men. And then he told me: "He is the boy who tortured me while I was at the Canal."

C.S.: *You have told me about him before.*

A.B.: Did I tell you how he had turned himself in to the *Securitate*?

C.S.: *No, you didn't tell me that.*

A.B.: I didn't?! So, he had stayed in Cluj during the period when the Northern part of Transylvania had been conceded, he had not fled like many others had done. He had done some extraordinary things, as a lawyer he had managed to save as many as possible.... He had helped those threatened by the Hungarian Police, and especially by the Hungarian Secret Police. He had been there for those threatened, it did not matter whether they were Romanians or Jewish....He thought of them as human beings and anyone who was in danger had to be helped. He had set up a network and thus, he was sending many people to Romania. At the same time, he had maintained close relations with the Romanian Delegation in Cluj and, if a Romanian leader was arrested, then he would announce it in Romania so people there would make, in turn, an arrest of an equally important person in order to make an exchange.

He had recorded all these stories in a book of memoirs, which I told you about before and which I believe should be published because they are very beautiful stories. When the war was over, he became an ordinary man. After the trial of the National Peasants' Party, the arrests had started. He had learned that a party member that had the same position as he did at that time had been arrested. And he knew that all the arrests were done at night with a compulsory ceremony: the cars, the slammed doors, inventories of everything there was in the houses, frightened children and so on. Therefore, one day, he had decided that, in order to avoid that ceremony, he should part from his family in a civilised manner. He had bought a winter coat, winter boots, underwear, a wooden suitcase with a lock and, having all the arrangements done, he went to the *Securitate* chief and told him: "I know that these people have been arrested. I came here on my own because I do not want to frighten my family." As nothing like that ever happened to him before, the amazed police chief said: "But you have not been programmed yet." So, my friend answered: "That's alright. I will just go to this hotel. Here is my card. You only have to phone me and I will come here by myself." He went to the hotel and after a week had passed without having been arrested, he went back to the police chief: "Sir, what are you doing? Why aren't you arresting me? I spent all my money and I do not want to go back home.". "You have not been listed yet.", answered the police chief puzzled. So he went home. The same night he was arrested with all the ceremony.

C.S.: *He kind of forced his destiny. Maybe he would have escaped the arrest. But like this, what a misfortune!*

A.B.: In the end, he got lucky. First, he was sent to Pitesti right at the time when Turcanu had started his sinister re-education. However, after a while, he was then sent to the Canal. He had been told that there had been a mistake. Fortunately, he had not taken that many beatings yet. That mistake meant his life. At the Canal, he used to be a driver. But his true passion were psychologic studies. He wanted to prove to himself that he was strong. And he also wanted to prove to others that survival was possible even in those conditions, that one needn't humiliate oneself, that one could fight and could find out what the exact political situation was outside, despite the isolation in which those people were forced to live. He had told me about some women who used to go to the cemetery that was close to their workplace. The women would be all dressed in black, would come with flowers and candles. They would start mourning their dead and then, in form of laments, they would start transmitting the news to the imprisoned, news about what was going on in the world. Or once he had told me about this woman who would find out when the detainees were transferred from one place to the other by train and she would run behind the train and collect the letters the detainees would drop, and then she would send them to their homes, so that their families would know that they were still alive. He had told me so many impressive things about a certain type of human existence. At the Canal he had learned to be a driver, job that he had also done after he was set free. While he was inside, he had made a moral classification according to professions and regions. As regards torture resistance, some of the Orthodox priest in his group came on the last but one position. Therefore, he had declared himself to be a free-thinker, and said that he did not want to have a burial service officiated by a priest.

C.S.: *You told me that he had arranged his burial by himself.*

A.B.: Yes, he arranged it by himself because he didn't have any family left in Cluj. Absolutely noone was still there. He had a friend, a former actress. His sister had left immediately after the war in Italy and his nephew did not even speak Romanian. I remember that he told me that he went once to Italy. They would not let him go, therefore he had asked for an audience to see the chief of the *Securitate*. "How could I let you go, you don't have any family left here. I have no guarantees that you will come back." "If I'm telling you that I'll be back, I'll be back." "Well, I don't have any guarantees. Who's going to pledge for you?" "Our boss!" "And who is your boss?" He used to be one of the most important people in the National Peasants' Party still alive: Ilie Lazar. He was someone that I had known extremely well and who, after he got out of prison, had been helped a lot by my mother-in-law. He used to have a poor hen, and he could not take care of it by himself, so he used to keep it at my mother-in-law's. He did not accept any kind of help from anyone. I remember that, in order to help him in some way but at the same time not to offend him, my mother-in-law used to put two or three eggs in his hen's nest every day. So, the owner would be amazed by how good his hen was. He used to be so innocent.... So, the boss pledged for him, he said: "If my friend promised to come back, he will return the day his visa expires."

C.S.: *And he came back.*

A.B.: He came back. He came back very troubled by the fact that his nephew did not speak his parents' language. He was born in a traditional family, a family of Transylvanian fighters, and it seemed strange to him that one of their heirs would not know his parents' language. His sister had made a promise to him that his nephew would come to visit Romania. He had made special arrangements for that. In his mind, there were a real Romania and the Romania of yesterday. He was a generous man who knew how to appreciate many of the things that were done at that time. I used to walk with him down town and he would tell me: "Look, these apartment buildings here will solve some of the housing problems." What I mean is that he was not resentful, that is, he would gladly acknowledge those things worthy of appreciation. And he used to keep telling me what a beautiful country Romania was and that his nephew, after seeing the country, would immediately learn the language. He had planned a very complex route for his nephew. But at the same time, he was feeling ill and had the premonition that he was going to die. His obsession was not to suffer, not to paralyse, not to become a crippled and make someone else take care of a dead body. From time to time, he would tactfully ask me: "Would you want to *help* me if something were to happen to me?". And he would start explaining to me that being intellectually crippled, not being able to work anymore, meant being dead already. What was the good to keep living? Feeding a dead body becomes useless. He wanted to imply that it would not be a sin, on the contrary, I would do him so much good if I helped him end his life in such a situation. He was simply obsessed with a possible infirmity.

His nephew was supposed to come but he was feeling worse, he had renal sclerosis, and I used to tell him, as a doctor, that it would have been much better for him to get admitted to a hospital. His mental mood had also changed. He was making arrangements for his nephew's visit, but, at the same time, he was making other arrangements as well. He had collected all his pension money, he had made a list with all the people that would need to have a drink at his funeral, there were around thirty people, he had written his obituary that was supposed to be published in both the Hungarian and the Romanian newspapers in Cluj, ha had payed in advance everything necessary for the burial, and he had also put some money aside in case something unexpected were to happen. He had the family tomb, so the grave was not a problem. Everything was arranged to the last detail. He had died in Brasov. That was his last trip.

I went to his funeral with a friend, Bodea was his name, who had taken care of his memoirs, had researched other people's biographies, people who had been in the resistence during the Vienna Dictate. He was the one who went to Brasov and brought him to Cluj. And then there was the ceremony. He had wanted to be burial service without a priest, because he was a free-thinker and all the priests he had known at the Canal had let him down in difficult moments. We found out that there was not any service for free-thinkers, there was only one for religious people and one for party members. So, we had to bury him with a priest. And During the ceremony I was thinking that his funeral was symbolising his entire life. He, who used to be such a fine man, always well informed about all the philosophic currents, he had been buried the way he had not wanted to. And the priest did not officiate a simple ceremony, but such a simplistic one that, if he had been alive, he would not have the patience to listen to it not even for a few seconds. While there were people crying, I could not help myself laughing hearing Cosbuc's verses recited with such a tremendous pathos: "From the forest you rip a twig / What does the forest care about it?". I think that even Bubi was dying with laughter up there in the sky.

C.S.: *We arrived to the end of his life story but you haven't told me his name yet, the name of this man with such a peculiar destiny, a man who had managed to face tragedies with so much courage.*

A.B.: Yes, his name is Aurel Socol and he was the deputy of Emil Hatieganu, the real, unofficial boss of the Romanians from the Northern part of Transylvania during the Vienna Dictate.

C.S.: *And because we got to talk about courage, I would like to say that Ion Marin Almajan, who interviewed you in 1980.*

said that, in his opinion, you would be the most courageous and true Romanian writer.

A.B.: Appreciations such as "the most courageous" should normally delight me, but I do not find them convincing. I always set my own internal, not external, goals. I know exactly where I want to go. I have a very clear imagine of where I want to go, I have a very clear image of the novels that I will write. I know how my future books should be written, and I am not only referring to the subject but to the narrative as well. What I mean is that, if I succeed in realising at least part of my mental project, I would probably have a very good opinion of myself.

I wish that time would pass slowlier, less permeated with events, that it would allow me to dedicate more hours to writing, to feel more relaxed, to think about literature not as a duty but as a joyful exercise. So far, I have always written under such pressure, that if I wrote with a pen, I think I would perforate the paper. I have always written furiously, rebelliously. I intensely wish I have more time, time to meditate about every word I put on paper. And thus, I believe I would succeed in realising some of the things I want to accomplish. I do not know when this time will come, or if it will ever come, or if I will reach this time I have been dreaming about, or if I could really use it.

C.S.: *And what if the most suitable mood for writing is precisely under pressure?*

A.B.: This could also be the case. I might find out that actually my normal mood is to write under pressure, that writing furiously is more useful than a sympathetic time.

However, I find this idea of courage that people are referring to not the most appropriate one. We have talked about this before, and I actually wrote a few articles on this topic. Courage for what? I do not believe in courage. I have always appreciated the idea of duty, not of courage. I am not courageous, I am an honest writer, but not a courageous one because I did not move any mountains. Writing about what is happening around us, emphasising those ideas worth dying for are things that belong to the category of duty, they are elementary things for a writer. In Romania, courage has become an aesthetic category, which I believe is false. Thus, I could possibly be regarded as honest, and I would consider any other attribute someone might use to characterise me pleasant and flattering, but only if I do not compare them with my own claims, only if I ignore my claims with regard to literature.

C.S.: *I would like to come back to that "under pressure" mood you are writing in. You told me before that there were also moments when you wrote with pleasure, not only with fury.*

A.B.: It seldom happened. I remember a Soviet film entitled "Nine Days in a Year". This is true for me as well: nine days in a year, I write with pleasure. As I said it before, I wrote *The Faces of Silence* in a kind of trance mood. It was an incredible pleasure. I also had these kind of moments when I was working on *The Voices of the Night*. Less when I wrote

Refuges and even less during *Vanities*. I think I have never written a book with such difficulty as *Vanities*. I mostly wrote *The Way of the Ash* with a tremendous torment as well.

C.S.: *You mentioned the novel* Refuges. *Almost all its characters are looking for a refuge. Did their creator look for one as well?*

A.B.: Oh, it is very difficult to say. In general, I have not looked for a refuge.

C.S.: *I supposed, well, I actually know from what we have discussed with other occasions, that there were moments of doubt, of restlessness, of dissatisfaction, moments when you do not foresee any solution. How do you react in these kind of situations?*

A.B.: It is true that there are moments in a day or a year when I feel like I simply cannot take it anymore. And then I take refuge in music. Music and travelling are my safety valves. With regard to music, every night, I listen to music for two hours to get ready for writing. Those are the hours I need in order to cleanse myself in a way, and to get into a working mood. If I feel very sinful and loaded, then I listen to Bach. When I feel very dry, very unemotional, incapable of putting two words together, I listen to Tchaikovsky, Rachmaninov, Mozart. But writing could be, and it actually is, a refuge to me.

C.S.: *One of your characters, Coman, confessed that there was a time when he would find great pleasure in writing, and that in the meantime writing has become a tremendous, excruciating torment. He was trying to write and could not get* *himself together. I presume that this was one of the author's feelings.*

A.B.: Yes. I am part of each character and each character is part of me. The author must identify with each and every one of his characters, must give life to them, but at the same time, the author must distance himself/herself from the characters in order to better manipulate all of them. Most of the times, I experiment with various moods. I tell myself: "How would I react if I were Coman?" and I try to transpose myself in those specific situations he is confronted with. I tell myself: "What if I were a driver and had an accident?". Thus, I must transpose myself into each character, I must live every situation the characters live. However, I must also have an overall image of all the characters, an imagine of the world they live in. Therefore, I am a bit of everyone, but I am noone completely. It is also true that I could have very well signed some of the essays Coman wrote. But I am not Coman, I am a totally different structure. I am all and noone.

C.S.: *The characters take refuge in love as well. Where does love stand in your writings?*

A.B.: Oh, this is truly a tough question! Writing about love is something that belongs either to literary maturity or to old age. For a professional writer, I think that the love scenes or the paragraphs that talk about love are the most difficult ones. A writer always risks to sound like other writers whose works had already read. For me, it is definitely the most difficult thing to write about. That is why at the beginning, in my first novels, I did not even have that many female characters. After a while, I said to myself: "Alright, let's give it a try." It was like a feat of strength. It is very easy to describe a murder, a death, a tense situation. But there are other requirements when depicting love. You need completely different instruments, and words, you need to seek inside yourself for what has not been analysed yet, to seek for those situations that you feel belong to yourself as a writer. This is what I try to do with my every book: not to repeat things that were already lived and said by others.

C.S.: *Which are the pages you wrote on love and you are satisfied with?*

A.B.: The waiting scenes. I believe that the waiting scenes are good, the checking out scenes during the walk in the mountains or at the house of that peasant woman, the three pages with Ioana's waiting.

C.S.: *What do you think that did not come out right?*

A.B.: What I did not fully succeed is to give the characters a mood beyond words, that is, beyond the description of the situation. At one point, I lost control of the book because I planned these three novels as a unity. In the third novel, I will have to try the impossible and introduce the 'living' mood, I will have to introduce those sentiments that live beyond the situation I was talking about. Exactly how I tried to do in *The Voices of the Night* when I described the feelings of those young people, who knew how to approve without denying. Love as temptation, love as waiting. I certainly was very unsatisfied with the novel's first scenes and therefore. I returned to them. Ioana is in a way the revival of Lena from *The Voices of the Night*. Only after I had finished the novel I realised that I had revived her on certain aspects. Which means that subconsciously I was unsatisfied. I usually return to various moods, to various situations which I consider to be unfulfilled in other novels. Or I return to various professions. For instance, I thought that the journalist in *The Faces of Silence* was unfulfilled, and therefore, I felt that I had to revive him in *The Way of the Ash*. Finally, looking back to what I have wrote, I realised that I always rewrote the same book, that I always retouched and refined the same characters, and the same moods. I sometimes feel like a painter that keeps perfecting his paintings and does not have the heart to let them go. I return, I return, I return, until I think it is better. This is how I am. The readers understand what they want to. They have the book, but I am left with the dissatisfactions caused by the book, dissatisfactions which I try to ease because otherwise I would not be able to move forward. It is all about this either very weird or very normal desire for doing better. And it is also related to the joy of knowing that I can surpass myself. If I did not set my mind to do more and more difficult things, I think I would not be able to write anymore, and I would not consider writing to be worthwhile. It would be very easy to write five or even ten novels about the same environment, having the same style as the book before, but I realise that it would become like a job, it would not be the work of a writer who respects himself. That is why I always change the approach angle, the perspective, the psychological types, in order to give myself that sense of difficulty that I need to surpass.

C.S.: *Do you give a certain significance to names?*

A.B.: No. They do not have symbolic meaning. I do not have key-names, names that by themselves would add a different explanation. This happened only once, in *The Faces of Silence*. I baptised the activist Rusu. But it was that activist's name that kept obsessing me, on the account of whom I almost got kicked out of college. However, they would not let me use it: Russians, collectivisation etc. They used to make a lot of connections, which in the censors' view "were not desirable" connections, but which, in my case, had not even crossed my mind when I had wrote about Rusu. Therefore, I transformed Rusu into Radu, to enter the same typographical space. However, the biography of this Radu has nothing in common with the Rusu that I had known.

C.S.: *In one of the issues from* Tribuna *from January 1985, during the nation-wide celebrations of the well-known event, the birthday of the genius etc., you wrote that this activist had been found dead. At the radio station "Europa Libera", we made some connections, some assumptions that maybe it was actually the same Rusu.*

A.B.: It is the same Rusu, but it was intentional. You guessed correctly. In this case, I was preoccupied with the idea of proportion, of imaginary and real dimensions a man can have.

When he disappears, when he dies, he seems to be a man like yourself. Apart from this, you imagine him to have frightening proportions. You are afraid to come closer, and to talk to him.

C.S.: *There was something else weird in that text. Rusu would ask people to come to him at 22.26. Does this have any connection with a real situation?*

A.B.: If you think of who I am thinking of, then no. However, it is a real situation from my village. This activist was taking care of the collectivisation. And he did not know what else he could have done in order to convince the peasants to sign up. He used to make their lives hell. He used to call people in to come and see him at these impossible hours. Peasants do not have this precise notion of minutes and seconds. They can barely manage the hours. Therefore, they all had moved in the courtyard of the town hall. Because if you might come at 22.25, he would punish you for being there too early, if you might arrive at 22.27, he would punish you for being too late. So, they all sat in the courtyard of the town hall. What I was interested in was this relation between the real man and the imaginary one. One creates a myth.

C.S.: *And death rearranges things in their usual places, gives them their real dimension back.*

A.B.: This happened to me too, when I went to Fontainebleau and saw Napoleon's bed. "Oh, my God, how small this bed is!", was my first reaction. Inside myself there was not the real Napoleon, but the man of his deeds. In that case, death changed dimensions the other way around. But a man stripped of history, of myth, is the same as all the others. What I mean is that, in the end, we all are human beings, and there is no point in hyperbolezing one or the other.

C.S.: *A few days ago we talked about moral decay and about the regeneration power of Romanians but unfortunately, we did not record it. We both reached almost to the same conclusion: that there are great chances for it to happen. In the meantime, I remembered one of your older observations: "the step from humility to dignity is even greater than the step made from monkey to man". Then isn't there a contradiction between the certainty that this regeneration power does exist and the affirmation of the difficulty of taking such a step? You know what I mean.*

A.B.: Yes. It is not easy to "reconstruct" a man at 50, at 60, or even at 30 years old, to restore someone on his/her normal foundations. But it is not impossible either. Something lingers on from the humility, the fears, the degradation, the limits imposed by terror. There are attitudes and moods that amass. No matter what, something still lingers on from all this. Even though the stress factors disappear, they remain in the subconscious. However, with change, man's concerns shift and there is the possibility of recovering something from what has been lost. Well, this is how I see it. Although I do not rule out another stress, other changes, even for the better!

C.S.: *What could be helpful for a moral rebirth? What is it that we need?*

A.B.: We need a smart view on history, on what is happening in front of our eyes. The truth about ourselves. We need truth and lots of knowledge.

C.S.: *A smart view! Romanians have learnt how to smile in the face of adversity and this is how they kind of fixed everything. They have learnt how to take everything* à la légère, *with humour.*

A.B.: With regard to humour, I think we have too much of that. I even wrote about it. This rooted conviction that to smile in the face of adversity is a great proof of superiority drives me mad. What is the point of facing history and not intervene in its mechanisms? I do not think that detachment is too big of a deal. I rather believe that an attempt to transform history is a big deal. If I stand on the side of the road and look at all the grotesque and ridiculous things that happen on the road and I do not do anything else but laugh my guts out, without trying to put an end to all that, I do not think that this is something to be admired for. Of course that there are a thousand and one reasons to laugh every day. However, given the present conditions, standing and just laughing I find it to be an act of irresponsibility. I admire laughter but not to such an extent. I could never live in a world *à la* Jarry, laughing all day long at Ubu. I think it is absurd. I am for intervening in the mechanisms of history. That is why I have written all those pages. I would not have solved anything by just smiling in the face of adversity. First, you have to get rid of the adversities and then laugh, if you can.

C.S.: *It has been said many times that laughter functions as a* *valve. Is precisely this function of laughter that bothers you, the one that hinders action?*

A.B.: Yes. This characteristics of our nation, smiling in the face of adversity, bothers me as well. I laugh with great pleasure, but I am not doing it in the face of our own adversity. Yes, laughter is a valve, but it is the most insignificant one. Revolt can be a valve. History must be confronted with, not avoided, one must not "feint" it.

C.S.: *You are a party member. When did you become one?*

A.B.: When everybody else did, following the Prague Spring, because it was a very good atmosphere. Many started thinking that one could have done much more good from the inside. Besides I was working in the press and one did not actually have a choice. The story was pretty simple. The chief-editor came with all the papers, I only had to sign them.

C.S.: *Who was chief-editor?*

A.B.: Dumitru Mircea. But, as I just told you, the atmosphere was very good. A promising environment for working creatively.

C.S.: *And now, looking back, do you think that this "quality" of being a party member was useful to you? If history repeated itself, would you still do it?*

A.B.: I would not become a member of any party.

C.S.: *Don't you think that a writer must be involved in politics?*

A.B.: Willing or not, one is involved in politics. I do not know exactly how it happened, but politics have become part of everything, from literature to family life, just like air. Unfortunately, politics have become the air that we are breathing. But back then, I did not have very clear ideas about what politics meant. I only had good-will, an enormous will to do good and an another enormous will to give out what was best in me. This way of being was also part of the medical principles that filled my heart and mind. Without pretending anything, because I have never pretended anything, ever.

C.S.: *Today, do you have more clear thoughts about what politics truly mean?*

A.B.: I have always thought about it, because nothing is left to be invented anymore. True democracy, real democracy, I do not know how to call it, is not a new discovery. The performances of the countries called democratic accurately demonstrate the advantages of democracy. Regarding reality from my own point of view, dictatorship actually means degradation and death. Man's degradation, man's humiliation, man's impossibility of freely expressing himself/herself and of freely create anything according to his/her own endowment. All dictatorships had ended ridiculously, but unfortunately, the losses they caused are immense, the traces left on men - sometimes incurable, the backwardness - difficult to recover. When I was mentioning those ideas about politics, I was referring to my place and my purpose in this deviant world of ours. I was referring to the fact that one must do everything, one must be a historic, a sociologist, must be there in the front row, well connected to and well informed about the literary performances everywhere, in the context in which material misery reaches alarming proportions. I was asking myself how was it better, but in the end, well, one does not have a choice.... and this waste hurts me.... One is judged by the book he/she writes, and not by one's heroic acts.

C.S.: *Who else became a party member in Cluj at that time?*

A.B.: I do not remember anymore. Anyways, many of the people around me had already left and went to Bucharest, like Ion Alexandru and Ana Blandiana.

C.S.: *When did you meet Ana Blandiana?*

A.B.: I met her when I was still a student. I used to go to the literary circle that was held by Zaciu at the Students House. Many of the editors from the *Tribuna* used to come there as well. And this is how I met Romulus Rusan, the husband of Ana Blandiana, who we actually called Doina, and we became friends pretty soon. We had different professions: he was an engineer, I was a doctor. I used to visit them very often. There was a very cultural atmosphere in their house.

C.S.: *Who else was coming to Zaciu's literary circle?*

A.B.: A lot of young people were coming. Paunescu was one of them. He was very young. I do not know whether he had already had something published or not at that time, but I remember that he was decided to do great things.

C.S.: *Have you seen Paunescu lately? What was the official explanation in Romania on his fall into disgrace?*

A.B.: I haven't seen him in a very long time. We had a friendship relation when he was very young, at the time of his debut with *Ultrasentiments* and *The First Lambs*, when he used to recite poems at Ana Blandiana's house. After that, there was a period when he used to do the mail at *Tribuna* and therefore, we had to talk weekly, when I had to send him the letters and he had to send me the answers. We used to talk quite often. I was very grateful to him for the interview he had taken me when I was down, after *The Absentees* had been banned. He had lent me a helping hand at a difficult time. As a doctor, I was amused by his innocence at the *Cenaclu Flacara*, when he would come out on stage surrounded by those charlatans, by those sorcerers, that he believed in.

I liked the fact that he had journalistic ideas. I respected him as a journalist, he knew how to write a magazine article, if he wanted to impose a certain point of view, he would surely succeed. Knowing my passion for journalism, he once told me, before he had been appointed at *Flacara*: "Would you come to work with him at a magazine?". "Yes, with great pleasure, with you I would do it with great pleasure." He had just published that book of interviews, *Under Question Mark*, a collection of very beautiful and very daring interviews.

C.S.: *Did he keep his promise and call you?*

A.B.: Yes, he did.

C.S.: *And why didn't you go?*

A.B.: I did not go because Paunescu has other rhythms, different from mine. I was thinking that if we were to work together and got into a fight, it would be a pity. And I even told him that. We might not have had the same opinions.

C.S.: *Where did this difference come from?*

A.B.: Where did this difference come from? He asserts something no matter what. I like to research it first, before affirming it. I like to hit the wall only if I can break it. To jog it and then come back and say that I took the wrong way, well, I do not like to do that.

We had not talked to each other for a while after that, I had not seen him for quite a long time. He had started the *Cenaclu Flacara*. I went to see two of his shows in Cluj. I was really curious to see how it all looked like.

C.S.: *And how did it look like?*

A.B.: He was ill that day and he was surrounded by different sorcerers. He was staying at the "Sport" Hotel. I told him: "Old man, why do you have to take them with you all around? Maybe they are good, maybe they are bad, but go see a doctor. I am not a doctor anymore, but I can still sense something. Why do you need this court?" This is one of the talk we had, the other one was when I asked him: "Do you really believe in what you are saying at the *Cenaclu*?" And he answered to me: "Yes, I do.". "Well then, I respect you opinion."

I saw these two shows and it seemed to me that he was doing something good as well, besides all the bad issues that people were talking about. There never was bad poetry recited at the *Cenaclu*. The poetry that the actors were reciting was of very good quality, first-rate. And, for those people who were believing in Paunescu, it was a useful phenomenon of spreading real culture. They were doing a good thing by reciting that poetry. And there was something else: they were promoting authentic folk music in a world where everything was perverted. The old songs were redone for the *"Cantarea Romaniei"*, and he was looking for folklore and old songs directly at the source. And there were also the patriotic songs, which, willing or not, play their role and are important when they relate to history. Apart from all this, I had never met his "court" which was encouraging him, and I do not know other details from his biography.

C.S.: *Do you think that Paunescu was really vying with the presidential couple? It was also said that he might have had a negative influence on Nicu Ceausescu.*

A.B.: I don't think he had influenced Nicu. However, there were tens of thousands of people present on his shows on the stadiums. And with them he would do exactly what he wanted. Up, down, left, right. He would shout at them: "You moved!" He would throw them out. The scolded one would leave feeling embarrassed. He was saying very harsh things sometimes, no matter that there was a representative of the local authorities in the front row. He had a strange power over the crowds. I do not know whether this is the reason for Paunescu's downfall. I only know that there were a lot of people objecting that he was corrupting the young, that he was keeping them there at night during the shows, that they were doing lots of crazy things on the stadiums. And then came the Ploiesti show which accelerated a somewhat predictable ending. I know that the rain caused short circuits, that the people crowed trying to get out and there were a few victims. I cannot say anything with certainty. This is what I have heard.

C.S.: *Let's go back to Zaciu's literary circle.*

A.B.: Yes, at that time there was a cult for Blaga. His works were passed around from one person to another in typed copies. He was still banned. People were also handing out his letter which he had addressed to the Central Committee with regard to the Beniuc case. Beniuc had ridiculed him in one of his novels, *On the Edge*, and, in response, Blaga had written a very dignified letter. The letter was later published by Zaciu. We were all aiming at doing big things. We were gathering foreign poetry that had been published in various magazines and we were putting them together in poetry volumes. I remember having a volume that I liked very much. I would see Blaga on the streets.

C.S.: *Have you ever talked to Blaga?*

A.B.: No, he would never talk. Once, I went with some friends at his house. He received us in the courtyard. We were looking at him, he was looking at us. I was admiring him from a distance. I would see him having coffee with D.D.Rosca. I would look at him and would say to myself: "That is Blaga!". When he died, I was in the clinic where he was hospitalized. I knew he was admitted there and I knew he had cancer. We wanted to go and visit him, but the professor would not let us. I remember that he was in Room 13. Professor Aurel Moga would not let us see him, not to disturb him, not to trouble him, but we would stand there on the watch until the doctor would visit him, the door would open and we would be able to catch a glimpse of him. He died in the hospital. We had planned on going to Lancram to escort the coffin. He was laid out in the hospital's chapel. Ms. Blaga was also there. Not that many people came. They were afraid. I did not go to Lancram after all. Ion Alexandru, Papuc and others managed to go, but I did not because on the morning of the funeral, around 6 o'clock, a guy came looking for me at the dorm saying that he was working at cadres. I told him that I knew very well the people at cadres, and therefore, he could have not been working there. He showed me an I.D. and he took me to the *Securitate*, where he asked me different weird questions until late that evening. At that time, I was not thinking about Blaga, I was thinking about my own sins, because, oh God, one only had to wish to find someone's sins and would definitely succeed. However, I had told my colleagues many times about Blaga. I used to always tell them: "You should go and see him at least now that he's dead. Such a great poet!". They took me in on grounds of all this commotion I had created. I spent the entire day at the *Securitate* office. I thought that they had taken me in for something else I had done the previous day. I remember that one of Khrushchev's speeches had been published in the magazine *Scanteia*, a speech full of biblical quotations. Someone came to me and asked me what I thought of the speech. I swore Khrushchev and said that he should know either the Bible or Marxism, but anyway, he should not have put the two together. That was his speech as a countryside mayor. Therefore, I thought that was the reason why they had taken me in. At the *Securitate* office, I just sat down at one table and the guy who had picked me up at another table. He asked me various unimportant questions and he would throw me matches every time I wanted to smoke. He asked me about Soviet films, about Soviet books, but he did not say a word about Blaga. And in the evening, they let me go.

C.S.: *And how did you figure it out that they had taken you in because of Blaga?*

A.B.: I just guessed, but I have no proof. Maybe it was for both reasons. However, I got really scared thinking that I might loose one year of college. This had happened to me before in 1959, when I had sung "Hora Unirii" in professor Hatieganu's house. A colleague of mine had climbed the statue of Matei Corvin, and then, we went to our teachers' houses to sing to them. We were singing freely for the first time. And then I found out that many of the students who had sung "Hora Unirii" had been taken in. Therefore, I did not go to classes for one week, I hid in the house of one of the drivers from the hospital.

C.S.: *You told me that many of the people who had been taken part in Zaciu's literary circle went to Bucharest, such as Ion Alexandru or Ana Blandiana. By the way, is it Ion or Ioan Alexandru?*

A.B.: Well, it's Ion. Initially it was Ion. Ion Alexandru had a successful debut. I remember being there at the circle's meeting when he had read some of his poems. They were very new, fresh, brilliant poems. I still remember some of the verses he had read then: "From the Neva, Aurora spits the saints in monasteries....". What a long way to the Ioan Alexandru of today. An extraordinary distance. We used to be very good friends in college, before he moved to Bucharest. He studied for one or two years in Cluj and then he transferred to Bucharest. He caused such a stir with his poems. And then, suddenly, after having finished German Studies, he turned to hymns. I do not know what happened to him. What I mean is that there are many religious people out there, but faith had not pushed them into writing such poems. He is a soloist, he found his own path, and therefore, I have no right to say whether he is good or not, but I can say whether I like him or not. And I like better the Ion Alexandru from his early period when he was Ion, I like him better than the Ioan Alexandru of today, of the hymn period. Anyways, Ioan Alexandru has become a completely different person than the Ion Alexandru I met in college.

C.S.: *Some time in 1982, you stated in an interview that one of your wishes was to move to Bucharest.*

A.B.: Well, what can I say, all my literary friends, except for Zaciu, Papahagi and Ion Pop, were in Bucharest. However, this was the main reason for desire to move. My entire life I had this idea haunting me, namely, that if I had been in Bucharest, I could have done much more than I was already doing, that I could have offered more than I already did. This was some kind of faith I had. I believed that in Bucharest I would have had a different efficiency, it would have stimulated me more. Furthermore, I had this obsession with travelling, no matter how little. This is a wish that had been fulfilled only now when I am old. I have always been sure of the fact that there were many things missing from my general culture, things that could have been substituted not by reading, but rather by experiencing them in person. There are important libraries in the world that I have never visited, there are cities that I should definitely see, as well as museums of course. And by living in Bucharest, I could have made this wish come true much easier. And there were also the discussions in the press, or at the Writers Union and so on. And if I wanted to take part at these discussions with my colleagues, I had to make a trip of 500 km. I could not communicate easily with them. It seemed important to me to be there where, one way or the other, a writer's destiny could have been decided.

C.S.: *I notice that you are using the past tense without having had your wish coming true.*

A.B.: Yes, for many years I had tried to do it. It was impossible. And now, even if the chance emerged, I do not know if I still have the energy to move. A neighbour of mine, a first sergeant, used to say that moving house three times equalled a fire. I had already survived two fires so far. And besides, my daughter and my son want to go to college in Cluj. I have consoled myself with the fact that one can do meaningful things even by living in Cluj. The difficult part is having discussions with my friends.

C.S.: *When we talked about* The Absentees, *you told me that the novel had a circulation of about 15,000 - 30,000 copies (you could not remember exactly the number). Is it a normal circulation?*

A.B.: One could say that. *The Faces of Silence* had a circulation of six or eight thousand copies. I called it a confidential circulation. It was decided to have a circulation of around eighty thousand copies, but the paper crisis started right at that time.

C.S.: *Was is real?*

A.B.: Yes, I believe it was real. All of a sudden the circulation of books, magazines, of all publications was cut down. I think the paper had been sold somewhere else. As for me, my next books had bigger circulations.

C.S.: *Did you have any troubles with the censorship with* The Faces of Silence*?*

A.B.: I had plenty of problems, but the book got away because I made various additions. I had to attenuate some words, to add some nuances, to make some explanations.

C.S.: *Did it take long for the book to get published?*

A.B.: All the discussions took long. I had very, very long discussions regarding the book. To some extent, I owe the publishing of my book to Mircea Santimbreanu who, at that time, was the director of the Publishing Department, I do not know exactly how it was called, but anyway, he was responsible for the publishing houses and he also was one of the directors of the Culture Council. I remember that I had a very long talk with Mihai Gafita. He would have published the book although he was not particularly excited about its content. But he had passed the book to Marin Preda. Preda had also kept the book for a very long time without having told me whether it was good or not. He only told me that it was too long. I went to see Preda and I asked him: "Do you want to publish it or not?". He told me: "If you cut out about two hundred pages.". "Why?". He said to me: "Even Stendal had cut out from....". "He did a bad thing.". "No, it's too long. It eats up too much paper. Come on, cut out some of it. I will give you a guy who can arrange it very well.". "No, I want to know what is it that you do not like about the book." "The size."

I told him that I was not going to cut anything out. He either published it like that or I would give the book up. He insisted that he was going to find someone who could adjust it without ruining anything, without the novel losing anything. And I kept saying no. And then, he came with the supreme reason: "Well, not even I wrote such a long book."

C.S.: *What was your impression of Preda?*

A.B.: I had many talks with him, but none of them was substantial enough, they were all superficial discussions about what we were doing in the Union's Council etc.

C.S.: *And as a writer?*

A.B.: I liked him as a writer. I admired him. However, I had my reservations as regards Preda the man.

C.S.: *I am interested in hearing about your reservations.*

There were two opposing currents of opinion about Preda: some admired him unconditionally, others argued that unconditional admiration was not productive and that it would be absolutely necessary to have a critical reevaluation of anybody's work, no matter the value of its author.

A.B.: No, my reservations are of personal nature. I would not want to be the person who breaks the monuments.

C.S.: *Was he a generous person?*

A.B.: He was, with some people. But not with me. He did not like me of course. Maybe he did not like how I wrote. Or maybe he liked it too much. I know only that we had never had a relationship, of any kind. In general, he tried to imply that he was too big for me. Anyways, I admired him as a writer. I have never had the slightest doubt that he was the most important Romanian novelist of that time.

C.S.: *So you did not accept any changes to your novel. What happened next?*

A.B.: The book reached Mircea Santimbreanu, and I had the most interesting discussion with him about it. He arranged a meeting with the representatives of the publishing house "Cartea Romaneasca", except for Marin Preda. There was Gafita, there was the book editor Georgeta Dimisianu, who fought a great deal for this book, and there also were some representatives of the Culture Council. I was very excited during that discussion. I remember that Santimbreanu took out a small notebook, where he had written down all my harsh lines from the book, the ones which were considered "anti", and he read each of them aloud and asked me: “What do you think of this one? And of this one here?”. I said that he could have found other lines as well, that each phrase taken out of the context had a completely different meaning, that, in that manner, one could have misinterpreted even “Lord’s prayer”. He told me: “You will have to give up all these phrases and you will also have to write another ending.” I said that I would have to think it over because, in the end, no one was making me publish the book, that I would put it aside for a while and if it did not resist a year or two, it meant that it deserved its faith. And I concluded that I was not in any rush to have it published. After the meeting was over, he told me: “You have to change the ending, because the character cannot stay undecided like this. Say something positive about collectivization. This character, the journalist, must make his mind about which of the two is better.” I said that I did not mind adding as many pages he would have liked me to, because making it longer suited me perfectly. And we did not come to any conclusions at that time.

We met one day, at a book exhibition at “Sala Dalles”. He came to me and said: “Hey, do not add anything to the book, who knows what stupid things you would do. Live it like it is, let’s see what can be done about it.” “I was thinking about adding some more pages, but I am not sure anymore whether I am going to have it published at «Cartea Romaneasca».” “No, no, come to my office to discuss this.”

So, I took the book and read it line by line, page by page. I would attenuate a word here, I would add some nuances there, but I did not change that much. Santimbreanu told me in the end: "You are lucky that I like the book a lot."

Fortunately, I had passed the publishing house level, and I had become a little bit more optimist, I felt that he really wanted to publish the novel. After he had given it back to me in the form it is today, I started running to editors and typographers to convince them to print it as soon as possible. In the meantime, the book was read by various people, from various institutions, including the Executive Committee of the Central Committee of the Romanian Communist Party. Back then, Ion Dodu Balan was the vice-president of the Culture Council, and he read the book. Mihai Dalea, from the Executive Committee, wrote a negative report, as I found out. What I mean is that I didn't have anything solid, but anyways, I started fearing that I was not going to see my book published after all. It was a very obscure business. At that time, at the censorship office, there was this Ms. Docsanescu who helped me very much.

C.S.: *You mean, the period before the "suppression" of the censorship.*

A.B.: Yes. I only met this lady after the "suppression" of the censorship, but I know that she was very understanding. If she had applied dogmatically the bans stipulated by the censorship, I think there would not have been much left of the novel and, of course, I would not have got the chance to have it published. Ms. Docsanescu, like Santimbreanu, also put some nuances here and there, attenuated the meanings of various words by adding epithets or approximations. However, the novel remained essentially how I had designed it.

C.S.: *Thus, you depended on the goodwill, on the intelligence and on the open-mindedness of the censor. A relation was established, which could have resulted in the denounce, the refusal to allow the publishing or the complicity, namely, the publishing.*

A.B.: It all depended on who would be reading the book. My luck was that both Santimbreanu and Ms. Docsanescu liked *The Faces of Silence*.

C.S.: *So, after the publishing house, the book would go further to the censorship. Which was the next step?*

A.B.: After the censorship, the book would go to the Culture Council, which, theoretically, was the supreme instance. But in "difficult" cases, the books would go all the way to the top people. The director of the publishing house also had a word in it. I only found out the story of the memos later. It was a way to escape responsibility at any level. There were rumours going around among the employees that the book was at this or that person, a critic or party activist. It was very difficult to discover the unfolding of the entire process. In my case, I was only allowed to speak to Mihai Gafita, the editor-in-chief of the publishing house. He was my contact person, who played the role of the intermediary between me and other instances, which I did not know about.

C.S.: *Today the process of publishing a book became even more obscure.*

A.B.: Yes, of course. Things are actually done at the Culture Council, where theoretically we do not have access. I for one have no idea who they are exactly, not even by name. And they do not consent to speak to me either. In what capacity? The editor-in-chief of the publishing house is the one who forwards me their opinions, what has to be cut off, what can remain unchanged.

C.S.: *Which was the book that you encounter the most trouble with?*

A.B.: With almost all of them. The only novel that had a "smoother" path was *The Voices of the Night*. And this happened due to an unfortunate incident. The book had been approved by Preda. Then Preda died and no one dared touch the book anymore. It was some kind of respect gesture for his memory. And I had the biggest trouble with *Vanities*.

C.S.: *You told me that an entire chapter had been cut out of the book.*

A.B.: Yes, e very long chapter. I usually do not give up. If the book does not come out the way I intended it to, then I do not publish it. I gave up this chapter because what interested me most had been left unchanged. The life of that character, Cristian, would have had of course more nuances. To a certain extent, his life has turned out to be linear because that chapter had been left out.

I would like to finish the story with *The Faces of Silence*. There were various protests arising. Santimbreanu would respond, because he had to respond to those guys reading it.

Anyway, the book finally came out. After the signal came out, I was summoned to the publishing house. When I arrived there, no one knew what was happening with the book. Then I found out that it was somewhere "at the top". I spoke to someone I knew at the publishing house and I convinced him to give me a bag full of books straight from the printing house. I did not even care what was going to happen next. I had seen the book published. I left, I called Santimbreanu up and I asked him: "Mr. Santimbreanu, may I give you a signed book?" Santimbreanu asked me: "But how did you manage to get your hands on them?" I answered: "Well, we are in the Balcans, where *tout est pris à la legerè*."

At that point I was waiting to see if the book might pass the Number One Cabinet. Then Jivkov came on a state visit. Everybody was involved with that. The waiting time passed, therefore, the book was sent into the book shops.

C.S.: *What is the waiting time?*

A.B.: I think it was somewhere between seven or ten days from the time it was printed. Normally I should have taken the signal-book, but someone else had wanted to read it.

C.S.: *Some kind of post-censorship. How was the book received?*

A.B.: The book received ambiguous reviews. Some said that I was idealising the peasant. There were discussions at a round-table in *Contemporanul*, where they tore me to pieces. But it did not matter anymore. The important thing was that I could have my book published. I should have read it one more time of course, because there were various parasite words that I discovered later, when I had the courage to take it and read it again.

C.S.: *It was said that neither Radu Gheorghe's nor Magureanu's attitude "concurred with the principles of socialist humanism".*

A.B.: Yes, I had it all: either there was one thing that did not concur, or there was another one, or another one, and so on. I already had the biggest shock with *The Absentees*. From that moment on, I became very aware of what I had to write about. I had not the slightest restrain anymore. I wrote *The Absentees* without any trace of auto-censorship. Actually, I have always considered myself free to write about what I saw and felt. I believe that no matter where I had been in this world, I would have written in the same way. For me nothing else did or does matter than expressing myself and be true to myself. As a writer, I had a censorship shock with *The Faces of Silence*. However, after everything that had happened with *The Absentees*, I already knew what I had to do. I cared about my opinion, and so I intended to keep affirming it no matter what. Actually, I became such a radical due to what had happened with *The Absentees*. I was interested in other people's opinions less, I knew how the peasant was, I knew in detail the history of those fights in the mountains, fights which I described only partially in the book, as in reality they had been much more complicated and brutal. I would have of course enjoyed also finding critics who had understood what I had intended to say.

But I knew that that was the truth, that was me, and the rest weighed less.

C.S.: *You said that with* Vanities *you had the biggest trouble.*

A.B.: I believe I was wrong in writing *Vanities*. I thought about this novel many times and, if I were to ever rewrite my books, I think that is the only one that I would actually rewrite. If not entirely, at least I would takeout a lot of things and I would add others. I believe that *Vanities* is a novel that I should have written only now. I did not have the necessary maturity for that subject. I do not say that it came out bad, but there are certain angles and nuances that I truly feel only now. What I mean is that, in the meantime, I had written a lot of articles about mental death, about death, life and love and all the other topics that were troubling me in that novel. And I did not only write about those subjects, I also profoundly meditated about them. If I were to write it now, and I do not know why but I am tempted to reread it, I believe it would come out differently. Only now do I feel prepared for it.

C.S.: *In one of his reviews, Dumitru Micu wrote that* Vanities *was one of the most passionate novels that had been published in Romania since the war.*

A.B.: I do not think I read that review. Yes, the book was indeed a great success. But I, as a writer, did not feel very good about it, because in the meantime I had the chance to read what had been written about death. Everything I could find in our libraries, *The Tibetan Book of Death*, *The Egyptian Book of Death* etc. I read considerably. And I believe that what

I discovered later would have suited that character, Cristian, so well, better than any other character. That is why I have this urge of rewriting it. Maybe it's nothing, maybe it's a false impression, due to the fact that there is that chapter missing, which we already talked about. And, every time there is something missing from a book, one has the feeling that has to add much more than the book actually needs. *Vanities* has always left me with a sensation of incomplete. However, I am sure that something is missing from the book, that imperceptible something which today I would be able to add to it. But it is very unlikely for me to ever rewrite it again. There is however a character that came out very well, that founder who always sends anonymous messages.

C.S.: *The book received very favourable reviews. Mircea Iorgulescu considered it to be "the novel of the confrontation between the primary spirit and spirituality".*

A.B.: Yes. This success gave me the courage to do something else. Initially, I did not want to actually introduce this founder character in the book, but I intended to write a book in the manner of the founder. And I will probably write it at some point if the topic will not grow too old. I have been toying with the idea of writing a novel in the manner in which the founder speaks, with all his imbecilities and his illiterate way of talking and writing. I had already wrote a few pages to see how it comes out, starting from a very strange idea that had popped into my mind at some point, namely, what might happened with someone living in Romania and respecting all the existing laws, and particularly *The Code of the Socialist ethics and Equity*, which has about 28 or 29 points. How would this person be regarded by the people around him? How would the others esteem a guy who wakes up in the morning, reads *Scanteia*, wants to help people cross the street, especially when they do not want to cross the street, a guy who feels "ideologised" to the utmost, who respects absolutely all the "indications"? I believe he would be a human oddity. In a world like ours, if one respects every rule, risks to appear as an absolutely bizarre character, from a different planet.

C.S.: *Do you think Romanian communists are winners?*

A.B.: Well, they are winners. They have the power! They do what they want! They imposed their rules!

C.S.: *You wrote somewhere that winners impose their own morale.*

A.B.: They try to do that. Yes, from a certain point of view, they won. In essence, they actually did not win.

C.S.: *So, in essence they did not win. Or....?*

A.B.: From their point of view, they won. They have the Constitution, the army, the police. They have everything. People do what the communists want them to.

C.S.: *If the communist regime collapsed, which is not that easy to happen because there is a certain mechanism that was formed there, a mechanism in which, as Alexander Zinoviev states, every wheel is geared with another one, but let's suppose that communism might fall, do you think that Romanians might still have regeneration strength left in them?*

A.B.: I believe so. I think that in just a few years, Romanians might catch up and even surpass the neighbouring countries. I believe it very strongly. This is a question I often ask myself and to which I also give an answer. I believe that Romania needs a few years to recover. I think that many experts falsely argue that Romania needs three generations to do it. I am convinced that the substance was not affected. I am convinced that the system did not play havoc with the deepest levels.

C.S.: *There is another thing which the system did not foresee. They do not realise that, by doling everything out, by limiting the citizens' right to express themselves freely, to travel, to have fun, to dress, to even comb, by limiting the television programme at only two hours per day, they do not give the people any other option for spending their free time, which is also limited by meetings, by interminable hours of sitting in a queue and by other "social activities", so they give the people only one option: reading. And people read everything they come across. And reading is a dangerous activity. I often see that the people coming from Romania abroad are very well informed and that their interior structure, in many cases, has not been affected yet.*

A.B.: Yes, their structure is very good. Of course that this is not everybody's case. Of course that there are nuances. Of course that there also are lost things, namely, human qualities and knowledge which are lost for a very long time.

C.S.: *What do you think that remained unaltered? What do you think that was either lost or turned bad? I do not insist* *on making an exhaustive psychological characterisation of the Romanian people here and now, but I have to admit that lately I have been wondering more often about the type of people we, Romanians, are.*

A.B.: An absolutely legitimate question!

C.S.: *It has been said that we are freedom and independence lovers. The present situation seems to contradict this affirmation. It has been said that Romanians seldom immigrate. And tens, if not hundreds, of thousands of people have already left the country. It has been said that Romanians cannot stand to be spoken to in a bossy manner. And for the last forty years this is how they have been spoken to. A friend of mine who has recently travelled to Romania told me that "the sweet Romanian language" has been transformed in some kind of barking. Romanians, friendly people who enjoy having guests, when are visited by a friend or relative from abroad, must declare it to the militia. Isn't it possible for some psycho-social features to have been altered?*

A.B.: First, I want to say something about what we discussed before, about our regeneration power. This is the first question one asks oneself: "What will happen tomorrow?". What will happen both with one's personal life and with the life of his fellow men. And therefore, one tries to see today's world and tomorrow's world. One tries to do it the way one can, based on the available data, not on scientific data because one does not have that, but based more on intuition, and on the contacts one has established with various people, if those contacts can really be helpful. I too have been wondering about our regeneration capacity because, I say it again, here in the West, I heard people saying that we need thirty or forty years to recover, that the country is destroyed, that there is not anything we can do about it anymore, that Romania is a country which does not interest the rest of the world anymore, let's say it, the rest of the civilised world.

C.S.: *The rest of the Western world.*

A.B.: Exactly. This seemed to be an aberration to me. An aberration which originates in the lack of the most elementary knowledge about the Romanian people. For instance, I am thinking of the Stalinism period following the war which brought all those tragedies, the Canal, the arrests, the forced labour, the collectivisation, everything it meant. At that time, a lot of intellectuals were practically taken out of circulation along with so many other people who had played an important role in the intellectual life of the country. There were a few left, in art, in literature, a few peaks which were nothing more than exceptions to the rule, and whose power and influence had been actually annihilated. However, there is something strange about our reality. We had definitely had much greater losses than the other countries which were also forced to accept communism. And I am not even referring to Czechoslovakia, where the taken measures had not been drastic at all, had not been as brutal as in Romania. Nevertheless, in 1961-62, there was a certain feel of freedom floating in the air, and we did not even know why because noone could have been able to predict anything. Well, in an amazingly short period of time, all the lost connections were tied up again, all of them, all the ties with Europe, with our spiritual past and our cultural inheritance. And thus, my generation emerged out of nothing, and I am not only referring to my peers in the literary field but in all fields. It raised by itself. And it created a creed for itself. It generated those books and research papers that today are still solid and worthy. In a relatively short period of time, out of scratch, my generation managed to create such values that are difficult to ignore today.

C.S.: *So, we should not doubt Romanians' capacity for regeneration.*

A.B.: When we know that a generation, which emerged after the catastrophes caused by the war and by what happened next, could recover itself, it would be absurd to doubt that the new generations would not be able to have similar performances. I cannot believe that everything is hopeless. On the contrary, I believe that there is hope, greater than it was after the war. It is impossible not to have much more important values, which will emerge tomorrow. The younger generation received a very good education, it formed itself during a period of strong contacts with the world. Furthermore, it learned how to always stay well informed. There are people who are up-to-date, and it is very hard to do it, very difficult and expensive. And these are people who, in normal conditions, could express themselves incredibly well and could definitely produce lots of surprises.

C.S.: *This is my impression as well. When I have a chance to talk to people arriving from Romania, as I told you before, I too am often surprised to see that the people are informed about everything that happens both in Romania and abroad.*

A.B.: Yes, absolutely. I know how I stay up-to-date. And I am not a rarity. I believe that in Romania there is an interest for literary prises higher than in France. There are foreign authors which have more readers in Romania than in their own country. And this is what I told Günter Grass as well, that I thought he had more readers in Romania than in Germany. This is actually the truth. There are so many foreign painters who are more famous in Romania than in their own countries. I think there is not a single important book that had been published in the West and not read in Romania, not a single artistic current or scientific phenomenon which is not known in our country.

C.S.: *So there is not a feeling of isolation in Romania?*

A.B.: Precisely this feeling of isolation is the force compelling us to make extraordinary efforts in keeping up-to-date. And, in the end, it turns out that we know more than the people we took the information from. What I am trying to say is that I do not doubt it for a second that Romanians know as much about culture as anyone else in any other country in the world.

I was at the Flammarion publishing house when they decided on the number of copies to be printed for a book by Moravia, a great writer, an eternal candidate for the Nobel prize. They could not decide whether to have three or five thousand copies for the first edition. In Romania, they would have hesitated whether to have three hundred or five hundred thousand. First edition! What I mean is that there are a lot of connoisseurs, or people willing to learn more. And one can find these people not only in Bucharest or Cluj or Iasi or... in any other big city, but also in the countryside. Furthermore, in Romania, there are a lot of dedicated supporters for sports as well, soccer, volleyball, tennis and so on. And they all are very well informed about what is happening in the West.

On the surface, Romanians are out of touch with what is going on in the West, but they are actually more in the West than any Western might imagine. Thus, the isolation theory is one of the falsest theories there is, and it originates in a superficial knowledge about the world. For instance, there are many journalists or writers who come as tourists in Romania. And we take them to see Maramures where they are impressed by the rugs, the houses, the Merry Cemetery. However, if they were truly curious, they would talk to the people and they would be even more impressed. The appearances are of course disastrous. One watches a film where they show frightening queues, snow mixed with mud, snow not lifted from the not-illuminated streets. All these are true. But if one talks to the people, will be amazed. I know lots of people in Romania who would make us proud in the West.

To answer your question, I do not think that there is all that much lost. If the West does not know us, this does not mean that we do not know the West. If ideas are not shouted out loud on the streets, this does not mean that ideas do not exist.

C.S.: *You did not tell me what is the role the radio station* "Europa libera" *plays in the Romanians' attempt to keep up-t-date. Which are the most popular shows?*

A.B.: *"Europa libera"* is the main means of information there is in Romania. I think it has the largest audience possible and a great influence. The news, *"Actualitatea romaneasca"* ("The Romanian News"), *"Teze si antiteze la Paris"* ("Thesis and Antithesis in Paris"), the weekly editorials.... People listen to everything, including music. It also has very good journalists. Hurezeanu, Munteanu.... Not to forget Anneli Ute Gabannyi, thanks to whom I met you. And to mention those who tragically left us: Noël Bernard, Vlad Georgescu, Cismarescu, Cioranescu. We, who are mentioned more often, we feel more protected. Our guarding angels think that we are agents working for I don't know who, and that we have terrible power. If they knew the reality, I think they would feel much better. I was often summoned at the Central Committee, where I was told to talk badly of this radio station. To write badly, of course. "What do these people say about me?", I asked myself. "They say that I have great value. I bet they say that! Then, how could I talk bad about them? Allow me to mention those who never said something good about me: *Scanteia, Romania Libera, Saptamana, Luceafarul* etc., well this is a different story."

C.S.: *My initial question regarded our moral regeneration* *chances. You mostly talked about professional regeneration, stating that there are people professionally capable to set the country afoot. I do not doubt that this will happen. However, I was talking about moral regeneration. Are there people morally capable to regenerate the country? Didn't communism exhaust certain reserves? Didn't certain habits become naturalised, habits which might make regeneration more difficult? Which would be the obstacles hindering the regeneration process?*

A.B.: Of course, there are many impediments. There is fear. There is mistrust. In Romania, people look both to the left and to the right when they talk. There is also the depersonalisation, the laziness, the apathy....

C.S.: *You are referring to the present. I am talking about the future.*

A.B.: Yes, of course. But later, if the system falls, each man can offer us any kind of surprises, extraordinary surprises. And it is the same with economic conditions too. People are tired, humiliated by misery, by the living conditions. However, the moment they would have the chance to let's say dedicate themselves less to the biologic side of their existence, to supporting their own lives in a basic way, the moment this would tend to become normality, then people would have more time to dedicate to the spirit.

C.S.: *Do you think that, to a certain extent poverty and misery affect the moral substance? Do you think that the generalised misery, which the people were forced to live in by the present* *society, can affect their character, can force people to lie, steal, deceive their fellow men? There is a certain fight for survival that annuls some values. Or am I wrong?*

A.B.: No, unfortunately it is true. The present society taught the people to be lazy. It taught them to cheat. It is terrible. Everybody is living in a world of compromises now. And in a world of barter. You receive food from the restaurant-keeper X. He does not need your money, but he asks you for a favour in return, for instance, he asks you to procure him car tires. Therefore, you have in turn to manage to make the man who has the car tires to be indebted to you, in order for you to get from him what the restaurant-keeper needs. Everybody, on his/her turn, must do all sorts of compromises. One enters a world of compromises where it is difficult to be oneself. Therefore, in this society, everybody is playing with their own lives, with surviving, with their biological existence, they do not have any other choice. But the situation will be different when these problems will not be essential anymore. It is terrible what is happening in our country, because the problem of having food is not something people think about once a month, not even once a day, but it is a daily concern, from morning till night. And this is not only one person's concern. And this is not the only concern. There are also other problems which are not easy to solve, such as having heat, clothes, or electricity. The electricity is being cut dozens of time every day. It is terrible. The moment these concerns will cease to be essential, people will not be forced to make compromises anymore. Suddenly, a part of each man will stay pure.

C.S.: *Do you think that these changes can happen just like that, automatically?*

A.B.: No, of course not. These mental shortcomings do not disappear immediately, but I strongly believe that when the element which supports them disappears or is lessened, then that place is taken by something else which people have inside themselves. Other facets of a man's personality are developing and then they come on first place. Because no one is willing to make all these humiliating gestures. People are doing them with restraint, with fear even. I am talking about people who are thinking of course. I am not talking about some kind of bartender who would automatically lose all his privileges.

C.S.: *As you said, there are certain people who are privileged by the communist society.*

A.B.: Sure, but I am referring to the butchers who would immediately lose their earnings. These people do not count in a society. Anyway, if all the factors of stress, all the daily horrors disappear, then there is a space left inside a man, a space to be filled by something else. When people know that they can earn enough to support their life projects, then they are not forced to steal, to cheat or to lie anymore. Because men feel far more worse, and far more humiliated when they have to make all those compromises we talked about. So, these would be my arguments: when the stress disappears, the mind remains free to be filled by something else. In theory, of course.

C.S.: *Communist society infantilised people, inoculated them, served them "false truths", which some people digested without thinking too much about them. Won't it be hard to teach people again how to think by themselves? I find it the most difficult task.*

A.B.: Of course, the most difficult thing will be to teach the people again how to think on their own. It will be so tough also because people used to entrust someone else the "task" of thinking and talking in their place, the right to be leaders of opinion. People "delegated" someone else to speak on their behalf. To change this, to make people think and take decisions for themselves will definitely be the most difficult job to do. Nevertheless, I believe, I hope that the Romanian people will manage to do it quite fast. Of course, there is so much that has been lost. Of course that due to the unilateral, deficient alimentation, due to all the chemicals and various types of substitutes, inside mutations have undoubtedly taken place, mutations that will become visible later, maybe even genetic mutations. However, regardless of these conditions, I still believe that nothing is lost for good.

There is a general thirst for peace, and by this I mean the peace of mind of having the bare necessities. And people are not all that pretentious, they only want a minimum material and spiritual comfort. I believe that it is possible to have this comfort assured, to have a new rebirth, more spectacular than any so far. I recall again how, in a short period of time of just about six years, between 1964-1970, we managed to recover the attained distances. I am thinking about the fact that, as I have said before, some of the best Romanian literary pieces were published in this period. And this happened even after 1971. That is, at a time when everybody considered us dead: cultural revolution, censorship. We had them both. However, those texts appeared despite the given conditions.

C.S.: *Would you tell me some names of authors who you consider to be the greatest or at least among the greatest authors?*

A.B.: They are so many. Thinking about poetry.... The order is absolutely accidental. There is Baconski, Geo Dumitrescu, Doinas, Blandiana, Dinescu, Malancioiu, Ion Alexandru, Cezar Baltag, Jebeleanu. With regard to prose, there are Preda, Stancu who is interesting for his literary picturesque, Breban, Balaita, Ciobanu, Banulescu who is very good, D.R.Popescu, Fanus, Uricaru, Grosan, Agopian, Cristian Teodorescu, Fulga. There are so many. And I wrong many others by only naming these authors who popped into my mind now. Of course, one can always make comments and criticise any of them in one way or the other. Of course that some of them made mistakes, but if one thinks only of the books and separates the books from the men who wrote them, then one can realise that books of great value were written.

developed an obsession with this award.

A.B.: Why not?

C.S.: *Who would think could be a worthy candidate? Who would you name for the Nobel Prize?*

A.B.: I have never thought about this before. If I were to make a comparison and think of the writers who already won this prize, then I do not see why Marin Preda would be inferior to any of the winners. For instance, I saw in *Lire* a few portraits of candidates to the Nobel Prize. Nichita Stanescu would not be in any way inferior to those who already won the prize. Or Sorescu, who is an extraordinary man.

C.S.: *Laurentiu Ulici published a book about the Nobel Prize. Have you read it?*

A.B.: I have seen it, but I haven't read it yet.

C.S.: *Well, Busulenga stated there that we lost out chance of winning a Nobel Prize with Blaga, if I am not wrong, and then with Marin Preda and Nichita Stanescu, precisely the authors you named as well.*

A.B.: If I am to think about it, we had the same ill-luck in between the two world wars. I am referring to Rebreanu and Reymont. I read Reymont and I really liked him, but Rebreanu was superior. I am also referring to a Romanian female writer who, if she had wrote in a different language, would have been famous: Hortensia Papadat-Bengescu. A first-class writer. Or Camil Petrescu. He is not in any way inferior to any other novelist who won the Nobel Prize. But still, we have this impediment: the language. Now, like in the inter-war period, there is the same situation: the authorities do not have the slightest intention of promoting Romanian culture abroad.

C.S.: *I think we also need a favourable political situation.*

A.B.: Yes, but still, the authorities did not invest in our culture at all. I have in mind this text written by Rebreanu a long time ago, where he was referring precisely to the diffusion of Romanian culture, actually its lack of diffusion. Today, this article still stands. What he wrote then is still actual. There are also some interviews which were published in the last volumes of his complete works and which point out to the same situation. Namely, the authorities are not making any efforts with regard to this issue. We can distinguish ourselves not by individually promoting this or that author, but by promoting them as a group, in order for others to realise that there truly is a literary movement in Romania.

C.S.: *Exactly. I agree.*

A.B.: Yes, we should do it the way the Russians did with their great writers. If ten Romanian novelists or ten Romanian poets are promoted at the same time, an interest for Romanian literature would be already established. There should have been, and there should be an intellectual and material effort. If in Romania one gathers various texts which have been translated in various languages, one could conclude that a Romanian author has accomplished something worthy. One might say that that author's work has been translated in many languages, but actually, to have been translated in Romania by Romanian translators does not mean anything. I am also thinking about that mania for anthologies which existed until a few years ago, but even this I think stopped being a trend. How can one make an opinion of a novelist when only three pages of his/her work have been published in an anthology? Or what about a poet who only had three poems brought out in an anthology? You know what they say, alright, that is it, we had achieved our goal, we had published an anthology of Romanian literature in a foreign language. What a great success! That is not a success, no one reads anthologies. All this trouble is just an expression of courtesy. The promotion of Romanian literature has to be done in group, not in anthologies. Each author with his own work. Now, I want to add a few words about the translation issue, something which I experienced first hand. There are no translators in Romania. There are not all that many translators in the West either, and anyways, they do not bother translating Romanian authors as the country is quite unknown to them. And they are not well paid for it either....

C.S.: *So, let's not forget that there is also the issue of funding involved, and that of finding an editor.*

A.B.: Yes. The moment they start translating Romanian literature, these translators take a risk. And a translator needs funding, needs support. In Romania, no one supports anyone.

C.S.: *What is there that could be done about it?*

A.B.: I think that one of the Romanian publishing houses could associate with a famous publishing house, they could thus collaborate by editing various books together. But even this project would need funding. What is there that could be done? We could affiliate to an important international award or we could even suggest the creation of a prize for translators. Such an award could offer us many advantages, and being an unknown country, there could be even more advantages for us resulting from this venture. A systematic long-term policy should be established. In Romania, there is this infallible list. There are this and that authors that need to be translated in order to be able to translate another one. But there are authors who are fit for a certain country and not for another one, there are authors who are fit for a certain moment, sensible only to certain circumstances. There should be an extraordinary flexible policy, which should promote as many authors as possible, starting from detective novels, why not, starting from the most insignificant works that could achieve public success in other countries. The idea is to turn writers from the most diverse genres into well known authors. What I mean is that we should not promote only certain authors. Let's say that Preda is not popular, although I think he could make it anywhere, then why not promote another writer, such as Grosan or Agopian or any other writer?

C.S.: *A lot of flexibility is needed.*

A.B.: Yes. There should not be a military hierarchy, neither in literature nor in the promotion methods. I believe that we need a systematic policy of promoting our national values. But rather than politics or anything else, we first need money. We need funds in order to put in circulation a few names. I have always written about my belief that culture is the most reliable investment. Where Napoleon did not arrive, Balzac did. Where Kutuzov did not manage to rise, Tolstoy and Dostoevski did. This is the most reliable investment, the most reliable way of getting to know a nation and also of its affirmation: its spiritual values. And their export. Cement has the same formula in Zambia, Romania and the US. Whereas the Romanian spirit is our patent and we can spread it anywhere we want.

C.S.: *But only if we make a financial effort in the beginning.*

A.B.: Yes, because later that Romanian spirit would make it on its own. And this is precisely the point that people did not and still do not understand. I am thinking about all the sadness of Rebreanu's texts and interviews. And today, as a writer, one is dead from the start. One has his/her country's quota.

C.S.: *This is what I was referring to earlier, the political factor cannot be underestimated.*

A.B.: Unfortunately, this is true. There is a very exclusivist point of view. If there is not food, then there is no spirit, and neither literature. This is a weird thing. For instance, we have some extraordinary painters. Since I have been in the West, I have seen many exhibitions and I must admit that in Romania there are at least fifteen painters better than everything I have seen lately. And noone knows about them. If one wants to go somewhere, he/she needs money. An artist needs money to be able to exhibit his/her works. An artist needs money to be able to transport his/her works. An exhibition space costs money. Our currency is not convertible, and one cannot accomplish too many things with those 75 pfennigs that one gets for a hundred *lei*.

C.S.: *Not to mention how much it costs to be advertised....*

A.B.: What can I say? We are on minus, infinite minus. Therefore, to return to the topic of the Nobel Prize, who could take notice of us? And with what? Who could be that benevolent person that would profoundly explore the Romanian cultural phenomenon?

The sad thing is that great values do not rise depending on any political criteria, they just rise anyhow. Although there might be the freest environment possible, there might happen that none of the expected talents or values or geniuses rise, and none is suitable for the historic moment.

C.S.: *What a sad thing it is for these values to rise and be ignored, and pass unnoticed!*

A.B.: Yes, indeed. I remember that at one point we had at least eight first-rate directors that could match any other famous international directors. Three or four of them became popular here in the West. But these directors had lived in Romania before, surrounded by sensational actors. Then why is it that nothing has been done about it at that time? Afterwards, it proved to be too late. The Romanian directors who leave the country do film editing for others, and all of them live with the nostalgia of the Romanian actors and say to themselves: "Oh, God, there are so many things that I could do in Romania!". Once I talked to Pintilie who is crazy about shooting films in Romania. He used to tell me: "I would at any time take the worst Romanian actress then...." How can I call her? Well, it's better not to give any names. These directors exist now. Tomorrow there might be the greatest democracy and freedom possible, but there might also be no Ciulei, or no Pintilie.

C.S.: *Nor Andrei Belgrader from New York, nor Tocilescu from Frankfurt, nor Andrei Serban.*

A.B.: Exactly. Talents live by different laws. God knows how they are born and how they disappear. Therefore, talents must be helped and supported while they exist. And it is terrible, if they rise in a time when they cannot affirm themselves. And the thing is that not all of them have the strength to fight. Today, one needs physical strength to write literature, one not only needs a certain ingenuity, but also biological, physical resistence. Not to mention other apparently small but essential things: writers do not have paper and pen, I do not even want to think about type-writers or computers, painters do not have canvases or colours. Poor painters, what they are going through with the colours they have! The colour runs on the canvas, or it changes colour, due to its bad quality. One is the light the painters see, and another one is the colour that appears on their canvases after a few days. What can they do? This is their tragedy. Tomorrow it might very well be democracy, maybe even the greatest of all, but we will probably miss all the names that I have already mentioned. But who knows, maybe others will rise.

C.S.: *We have been talking about the authorities' lack of interest in promoting culture, their lack of concern for the problems of the cultural man. However, there also are those who are in the position to intervene and improve this situation, but who still do nothing about it. There has not been a meeting at the Artist's Union for almost fifteen years, I think. There is a state of neglect.*

A.B.: Neglect yes, but if they had the necessary money, they could be competitive, if they were allowed to, they would not need the Union anymore, because we have to admit that there is a spirit of competitiveness in each and everyone of us. If each of us did not think that he/she is or could be the best, then we would not exist anymore. And there is another thing too. Today, there is impossible to talk about a writer with sincerity, there is impossible to value a writer with that serious and pharmaceutical measure of a highly competent critic, because that writer is brought then to light, but to an awkward light compared to the nullity sustained by many of the magazines. And then, the critic has to affirm the best writer, although his/her latest book has many deficiencies. The unit of measure has been lost. The good and the bad have been mixed. There is not a real hierarchy of values anymore. And this affects everything. Of course, there is the Writers Union and the Artists Union, and of course that in the way they are organised, they both are good enough for that minimum that the majority needs. But in a democracy for example, there is a need for a truly literary press, where opinions can be exchanged, where issues can be stated and contested, where the normal appreciation criteria can function properly. I wonder what would happen if the Romanian literary life or the overall Romanian situation were analysed only by reading what is being published in the newspapers or the literary magazines. One might get scared. Or even worse, one would not understand anything. There is no more press, and for a writer this is a terrible reality.

C.S.: *But don't you think that, when things will return to normal, many people will enter a state of shock?*

A.B.: Sure. The idea that *it is impossible* is comforting for many people. Absolutely. And when they will have to fight....

C.S.: *By normality you mean real competition.*

A.B.: Real and very tough competition. Exactly. So, for many it is very comforting that things cannot be done, for them it is very good that things are impossible. They curse, but they are essentially composed. Others find refuge in the most art-for-art`s-sake theories, which are past history in the West and are new only to us. This is a very dangerous somnolence of the spirit. I wonder how will they wake up. I was thinking, it is not related to what we were talking about, that during the Prague Spring there was this first-rate journalist who rose and who I had not even known that existed before. His name was Eugen Ionescu. He used to write incredible reports about the events in Prague during the Russian intervention. Amazing reports. I do not know what happened to him later, as he just raised from nowhere and was put in the position of truly doing his job in a historic moment.

C.S.: *And he managed to do it, as I understand.*

A.B.: Stupendously. I would have rather listened to Eugen Ionescu from Radio Bucuresti then to anyone else.

C.S.: *Three days!*

A.B.: Three days. But the story was astonishing.

C.S.: *Anyway, what a chance he got to live at least for only three days the life of a true journalist!*

A.B.: I too lived for three days as a true journalist.

C.S.: *Where?*

A.B.: In Cluj, during the same period, when I was doing live shows on the radio. What was so amazing was that all the right words were just popping in my mind, I did not have to look for nuances. And I felt very good talking live on air or writing exactly what crossed my mind. Maybe journalists that we do not know about will appear, and names that we got used to will fade away.

C.S.: *The truth is that people do not remember the names of any journalists. The regular man just reads an article, if he/she succeeds to do that, and does not bother to see who the author is.*

A.B.: Yes, while abroad every big newspaper has its own columnist. However, the people who swung between truth and lie will suffer the most. Yes, a little bit of truth here, a little bit of lying there, until not even they knew what reality truly was anymore.

C.S.: *I have a strange feeling while we are sitting here and talking, as if, by talking, we are bringing change about.*

A.B.: I don't know, I am not very optimistic.

C.S.: *You should be. You once stated that your novels are optimistic.*

A.B.: They are optimistic. But I have always had a few simple ideas. I needed twenty years to rediscover that, in the end, the novel is *character* and *construction*. And today if I were to tell this to our great aesthetes, they would consider it an old concept. They could even reproach me that I am returning to the traditional novel. But I am in no way writing traditional novels. I still have the conviction that the character has to exist no matter what, no matter how many metamorphoses the novel would sustain. Every time I create a character, I have the same feeling I had when, a long time ago, I used to sculpt. Today, I sketch the forehead, the chicks, the eyes. Tomorrow, the hands. I will look for the character's expression until I am able to actually see the character. So, every day I add to that character something of what I have and carry with me everywhere: a nuance, a line, a particularity, until I see that the character is alive. I have to have exactly the same sensation a sculptor has when his work is done. Of course, a work out of the best quality material. When the character is ready, I part with it, that is, I put the character in the novel. But at the same time, the character becomes my partner, one of my peers who accompanies me everywhere and, a very strange thing, forces me to always take it into account, until it drives me mad. Now I am in this phase when all the characters in *The Wall of Death* drive me mad, and I am finishing this novel, and I do not want to ever hear about this *Wall of Death* or about any other novels with sequels anymore. These books are too old for me. They are ten years old. I have to already add them in my passport. They have been terrorising me and bored me so much that I am forced to get rid of them as soon as possible. I even had to kill a couple of them because I could not stand them anymore. I do not like to kill my characters, but sometimes I really have to do it.

C.S.: *I noticed that when the characters die, it is not all that certain that they are not going to come back till the end of the novel. I do not remember if I read this somewhere or I just thought about it when I read your novels, but it seems that some characters which, as you said, you had killed, continue to live even after death. They had died but still there is a certain* *shadow of doubt floating around their death. This is the case of David Helgomar. One keeps asking oneself whether he really died or not.*

A.B.: He did not even exist. Victoria is dead. I cannot either kill or resurrect Helgomar. I have to leave it like that because he is just an idea.

C.S.: *The* Securitate *tells Victoria that his grave is right over the border, that he was shot by the border police while he was trying to cross the border to Hungary. Is it like that?*

A.B.: Yes.

C.S.: *However, he reappears at a certain point and says: "I am Helgomar, I am alive. Victoria is crazy, I wanted to get away from her, and then I left and moved hundreds of kilometres away to get lost". But there still remains a shadow of doubt around him.*

A.B.: There is also that mad-man who keeps appearing and repeating like an automat: "In the last forty years...", he kept repeating the same phrase over and over again, no matter what one asked him. Thus, he can be any of those who appear and disappear, those persons that we do not know whether they are dead or alive....

C.S.: *You turned him into the symbol of rebellion.*

A.B.: Yes, the symbol of rebellion and the symbol of a different way of living in freedom.

C.S.: *Because we are now talking about rebellion, I wanted to add that for you it is essential to tell the truth. Telling the truth becomes synonymous with rebelling. Or am I wrong?*

A.B.: I believe that noone knows the truth, but each and every man must tell what he/she is and thinks, because the truth is the sum of all these opinions. In life, there are so many truths, but there are also generally human truths, which are compulsory.

C.S.: *Is this the point of view of the journalist in you?*

A.B.: When I am writing articles, I start from a different perspective. I could tell you so many things about journalism, because actually, I am also a journalist for the sake of a few formulas which need to be imposed, explained, deciphered, always taken from the beginning - like a teacher who needs to always start from the beginning with each and every of his students. In my texts, there are a lot of repetitions.

C.S.: *I have noticed that. Insistence on telling the truth as a way of educating others.*

A.B.: Well, I do this deliberately. I do it because when I wrote the text, I knew that it would be useful to those who would read it. I want the text to be useful to them. And therefore, I repeat obsessively: truth, truth, and some more truth. Why am I talking so much about truth? First, strong people have nothing to hide. When one hides something, one is weak. True people have to say what they believe, what they feel, what they think, because only if there is a free dialogue, one can move forward. When I have all my cards on the table, I can persuade you or you can persuade me. If I do not tell you who I am and you do not tell me who you are, then it would be like two blind people playing tennis.

C.S.: *So, the message would be: "Tell the truth because only by telling the truth one becomes strong, and free".*

A.B.: Yes, one becomes free. And if one wants, even just a little bit, to hope for and bet on the future, then this cannot be done with crippled people, with people who have not been used to telling the truth. I try to educate, if you want, let's say, I try to educate the people of the future.

C.S.: *And which is the perspective of the novelist?*

A.B.: With regard to my books, if I read what I wrote, I sometimes think that I took the most wrong road possible. But I have told myself that between writing whatever I felt like and please myself, and writing what is necessary, I have to choose the second option. I wrote what I thought it was necessary to be written.

C.S.: *What were you tempted to write?*

A.B.: I was interested in writing experimental novels, science-fiction novels, and especially, psychological novels. And well, I had to always give up one thing or the other out of this need to fulfill my mission.

C.S.: *Do you consider writing to be a mission?*

A.B.: It is all about this Transylvanian lunacy. You have to do your duty, even if you lose.

C.S.: *How can you know when you lose?*

A.B.: I feel when I am losing. For instance, I have always lost when it came to journalism or interviews. I have always repeated the same thing over and over again because I thought it was necessary at that precise moment. I have never thought about, or actually, when I am thinking in general, I do not particularly like this obsession of usefulness. But I have always been so anxious to be useful that I gave up many things I had inside. That is why I want to finish this cycle, *The Wall of Death*, to free myself from journalism and write something for myself as well.

C.S.: *What would you like to write?*

A.B.: I want to write a book I like and not to feel forced by a real or imaginary contract to finish the book....

C.S.: *The characters in your novels make confessions, they leisurely explain the reasons for which they reacted one way or the other, what forced them to make one or the other gesture. I had the impression that thus they tried to save themselves from a real or imaginary guilt. Often imaginary.*

A.B.: This is in a way the conclusion I reached by having read old literature, getting to know religious literature and practices, and later, psychoanalytic practices. One can move forward only after having confessed. One can know where to head to only knowing who one really is at a certain moment or at a turning point in life.

C.S.: *You are not offering your characters the chance to choose, the destiny that you planned for them is inexorable like in the Greek tragedies. Why don't you give them a chance?*

A.B.: I give the reader a chance.

C.S.: *For many of the characters, confession comes too late. Confession is not a salvation instrument anymore, but it turns into a history lesson.*

A.B.: Exactly, a history lesson. Indeed. This is what I learned by having studied the great authors. In Dostoevski everybody confesses, on hundreds of pages. In Proust or Joyce, the same thing happens. There are moments that force you to confess. The moment of taking a decision, for instance. The moments of confusion, when you do not know who you are anymore. You have then to look inside yourself to find out who you were. Confession moments are crucial in a person's life. And it seems to me that, the more you confess, the more chances you have to understand and decipher your destiny.

C.S.: *It may be so, but your characters not only confess, but they also justify themselves. They justify almost every step they take.*

A.B.: Yes, because they have a faith. Good or bad but it is a faith. And the characters justify themselves with regard to certain convictions they had the moment they took action, and with regard to the cause they found themselves associated to.

C.S.: *Is justification proof of the character's evolution?*

A.B.: It is proof of its change. Proof of the fact that the character can be different, but if he/she buys a train ticket on a certain route, he/she has to go exactly on the same route as the train, and then he/she has not any other choice but to watch the scenery.

C.S.: *Forced by the route the train goes on?*

A.B.: Yes, if he is a communist, then he has certain compulsory rules to follow. The moment he tries to understand those rules, according to which he has taken action before, which had compelled him to react in a certain way, he might discover that the route he has been taking and which seemed good to him before, is not actually the true route, he might discover that there are other solutions as well, other routes. My characters scrutinize the existing information and facts only when they are forced to make a choice, only in the dramatic moments. And of course, not all of them do that.

C.S.: *Which is the character which you find closer to you?*

A.B.: What am I going to tell you might sound very strange, but I have this feeling of certainty - and it is terrible because it would have been better if it were only an impression -, I have this feeling that I have not yet written the book to represent me. The character I find closer to me? Maybe it is not yet born, maybe it will be when I write the book I dream about. I always have this feeling that this book which will represent me, in which I will fully express myself, is still to be written. And so, I focus on three, four books which I have already outlined in my head. Those books that I had already written do not interest me anymore. If it were not for the let's say disagreeable destiny of *The Absentees*, situation in which both the book and me personally were offended, I would not be interested in it at all. Look, there are twenty years now since the book was published, I did not ever read it again, I did not even skim through it again. I did not ever reread any of the books I published, I think that the only exception is *The Faces of Silence*, although in some cases I should have done it, at least because of all the printing mistakes which would have needed correcting.

C.S.: *Have any of your books been reedited?*

A.B.: Only one, *Vanities*. And I am terrified by the moment when another one will be reedited and I will have to reread it again. I try to forget all about the books I wrote in order to have enough space left inside myself for the books I am thinking about. However, I don't go back on any of my books or anything I ever wrote, not even on my debut book. That was me at that precise moment, that was all I was capable of at that time. Noone ever forgives you under any circumstances, no matter whether you have been a coward, or just frightened. Therefore, I don't see why I should find excuses for any of my books. And I don't want to place each of them in some kind of context either. A book, if it really is a good book, then it has to live, it has to survive the moment of its publishing. If it is not good, then it may very well die.

C.S.: *What is important to you as a novelist?*

A.B.: All I care about is to be satisfied with knowing that I did everything I could, that I expressed myself, the person I was at that time. And that I did it in the best way I could, as much as my mind and talent helped me. I do not like excuses, or apologies, I do not need anybody else's understanding for the context I wrote in. My biography does not matter at all. I am my own books and that's it.

C.S.: *Do you attend the meetings with the readers?*

A.B.: At the beginning, I used to go more often, but now I almost never go. This is something that I have never enjoyed doing. I am not a verbal guy. I don't have anything more to say than what I wrote in my books. When I find myself in front of the readers, I feel like an awkward exhibit. I think I wrote my books very honestly, or at least, this is my conviction. In each book, I said everything I had to say, and I, as a physical person, do not matter. That is why I don't like meeting the readers, I am not spontaneous and I don't feel the need to give more explanations than those that can be found in the book. I don't feel the need to talk about my projects, and to answer in the place of those responsible for why are the editions so limited, or why are there things missing. Let them ask them, and other things as well....

C.S.: *Who in the literary world do you find closer to you?*

A.B.: Oh, there are so many people that are dear to me. I have already named a few before: Zaciu, Papahagi, Ion Pop, another poet from Cluj, Vasile Igna. Tudor Vlad too. I also am very close to Laszlofy Aladar, a very good Hungarian poet, and to Szilagyi Istvan, an excellent fiction writer. These are people that I am very attached to. There is also a very good Hungarian critic, Kantor Lajos. And a young poet, who I believe will have a great impact on poetry: Ion Muresan. Bringing this young poet to the editorial staff I think is one of the positive things I have done since I have been working at the *Tribuna*. He is a poet of great talent. And I hope he will evolve in a fortunate way.

C.S.: *And among those in Bucharest?*

A.B.: I am fond of Manolescu, Ornea, Blandiana, Mircea

Dinescu, Paler, Paleologu, Haulica, Eugen Simion. And I have a strong feeling of gratitude to Valeriu Cristea, which keeps me from being very close to him.

C.S.: *You once wrote that noone can be forced out of the literary scene. Do you still believe it today when Blandiana, Dinescu and many others have been banned?*

A.B.: Yes. They can only be banned for a short period of time. But it doesn't mean anything. Besides, we shouldn't forget about the Balkans....

C.S.: *Don't you think that these intervals, no matter how short they are, have a traumatic effect on these people, and even more than that?*

A.B.: Of course that they are affected, and traumatised. But on the other hand, I say that, if one starts writing, one must know that it is a very dangerous job and has to assume all kinds of risks. So, the risks have to be reckoned, even the risk of being banned for a while, even the risk of having to suffer. Some have been killed. I am thinking of Mandelstam or Babel. Literature is something of great responsibility, if done seriously. A writer becomes a public person, an institution. And therefore, the writer has to answer for his/her every written word.

C.S.: *What do you mean by this?*

A.B.: What do I mean? What I mean is that a writer has to answer for his/her every written word, for every produced statement. Unfortunately, in Romania, sometimes, actually very often, one has to speak in the name of others. One is forced to ask in their place all the questions that they either lack the courage to ask, or they don't know how to or can't do it by themselves. So, risks have to be reckoned. When a writer has taken this path, knows what awaits for her/him. If one follows the line of least resistance, then she/he is exempted from emotions. But if one does his job right, the way its unwritten laws require it, then other things come into play, such as being banned for a while, or having to suffer, or even death.

C.S.: *What do you think about Dinescu's gesture of giving that famous interview for a French magazine?*

A.B.: He said what he thought. I find it a normal thing to do. It is the poet's right to say what he believes. And anybody else's right as well. I would hold myself cheap if I hadn't believe in my right to say what I think. So, I take my hat off to Dinescu.

C.S.: *Don't you think that there are still far too few people using this right they have? Don't you think that there shouldn't be any more individual manifestations but rather group actions? Maybe there are historic moments, like the one we are experiencing right now, when limiting yourself to only saying the truth, and even to writing literature, is not enough anymore, don't you think?*

A.B.: I believe the exact same thing. I don't have anything else to add to what I have said before. I would like to articulate some nuances though. I do not have an answer to this question. I do not know which is the best solution. I believe that we as single individuals have to do our best, as much as our talent and conscience help us. Then, I think that we cannot ask the same thing from everybody: some are of great endurance, others of such a frightening fragility that one cannot touch them with a rose. I believe that within a country, within a culture, there must be a place for everybody. Some are very old. Others are sick. Both physical resistence and biological resistence are influencing factors in all these confrontations. This would be one of the nuances I wanted to state. I got to know so many people and I had a chance to sit and talk to them. I asked them and they answered me: "I cannot. I cannot hold out anymore.". I can understand this too.

However, there are other things that I find impossible to accept, namely that one is not allowed to make or accept compromises in the name of certain physical or moral weaknesses.... for the sake of the children, for fear of miseries or poverty. But it is impossible not to take these weaknesses into consideration, although they don't give you the right to behave in this job in any way differently from how you should.

C.S.: *Don't you think that the reasons you stated can often be used as excuses for not taking a stand? Don't you think that in Romania the intelligentsia remains, with a few exceptions, passive, indifferent to all the suffering around them, and sometimes even to their own suffering, which is totally incomprehensible?*

A.B.: The intelligentsia is not passive. This is a mistake. But I would like to also further develop the issue I have discussed before.... I know what to ask of myself. There is still one question to which I didn't answer wholeheartedly and which forces me to reach a rational, logical conclusion, based on a solid argumentation. This question is: "What is more useful? What is more moral and correct: to write my books leaving aside the uproar, the agitation, the idea of usefulness, or to choose the path of open confrontation? How many people will follow me? How many people strive today in practice, not in theory, with books, and not with lamentations such as *it cannot be done, they don't let us do it* etc., how many strive today to confront the authorities, the "inexistent" censorship, all the *politruks*, those political instructors? The great lamentation - without real books, without any kind of texts - also conceals a lot of cowardice, a lot of hypocrisy, a lot of fear. The courage of many courageous people is often limited to writing a letter to D.R.Popescu, the president of the Writers' Union, when they should set their target much higher up. Who stops them from at least trying to fight the System through books? There are some who criticise me - and they are not a few - arguing that I endanger the Literary fund with my writings. I should not write anymore? I should let so many wonderful colleagues starve and fear?".

C.S.: *May I say something? Augustin Buzura is a first-class writer, with a well-established reputation, a writer who can afford to state things which others cannot. That which is normal to you becomes a luxury for others. Do you really think that they, the "wonderful colleagues", enjoy the same treatment as you do?*

A.B.: I don't know. I believe though that it is a writer's duty to defend what she/he wrote, namely, those few essential ideas which she/he believes are worthy of being defended no matter what the cost.... This is a fight which writers should carry with more energy than they do. Of course that now I am able to say more than others can afford to. As someone said, I should have been killed when I was young. But I have not stopped since the day I had discovered what I had to do. At that time I was as famous as they are today. On the contrary actually, when I debuted, most of my generational peers had been long well-known. As I have told you before, I had to work very hard in order to manage to catch up with them. What I'm trying to say here is that I too rose out of nothing and in the same conditions. And as long as I have managed to keep telling the truth, I don't see why others cannot do it. This is how I think now.

C.S.: *But still, the situation was different in the 1970s.*

A.B.: Many things have changed, I admit it. But the situation was not all that comfortable either. I have been fighting for every book much more than I did at that time, a long time ago, when I had my debut book published. I think I have told you this before: it took me much more time to have a book published than to write it. However, I am still not done with this obsession: what is more useful, literature or journalism? Today, one is being judged more according to an article or a protest than to a twenty-year-old work.

C.S.: *I don't understand.*

A.B.: I am talking about the way a Romanian writer is looked at here in the West. They don't care about what I have been doing for the Romanian culture for the past twenty years, they don't care about the books I or someone else wrote, but I would be a very important person if I were to write an article entitled "Down with this or that!". Down with someone that they defended before. Yesterday, of course.

C.S.: *Who is "they"? Who are you talking about?*

A.B.: They, the people from the West. You know that I have been talking to many journalists here in the West, to political figures, to important writers. They keep asking me "Why don't you step into the ring?", and I ask myself bewildered: "But what I have been doing till today?". And I believe that in my novels I said much more than all the journalists together. I said exactly what needed to be said about censorship and dictatorship. Actually, if I had to say something now, I would not have anything else new to add. This is one thing.

The other thing, and this is related to my personal pride, is that I do not want to distinguish myself with any other means than that of a writer. I do not want to distinguish myself as anything else but a writer, with the product of my literary work. The moment I would write for the Western press, and my books would be translated here, I would be able to move more easily, without all those material difficulties that I encounter right now, I would indeed be well-known. But these are precisely the reasons that stop me from doing it. I risked everything, all the comfort related to my own life. And I did it for the sake of this job. I did and I still do this job wholeheartedly. This is all I can do. I cannot do more than this. I loathe the ignorance of the people in the West. I do not want to be useful to the people here. I know that I am useful at home, in Romania. I think that a book in which I said everything I had to say is more useful than an article which would make me famous here, but would stop me from being published at home. I do not need Ceausescu's help, I do not need this vector to be known here. When someone will manage to convince me that a newspaper article is more important than a book, I will give up. I don't know if you understand what I'm trying to say here.

C.S.: *I do, but I think that this is just one part of the issue.*

A.B.: You know that I am a democrat, maybe not the most convinced one, but anyway, I am a convinced democrat. But I believe that Blandiana is still very good even without that famous Tom-cat. If I were to step out from novel writing, I would enter a territory that I don't particularly like. I do make politics through what I write. Every text I have ever written has a political side to it as well. I know that noone here in the West agrees with me and they keep telling me "You have to step into the ring!". But I have been in the ring for the past twenty years, didn't anyone notice me?! Maybe I will get to the point when I will do the gesture people are pushing me to do right now: curse Ceausescu. But I will do it only when I will not be able to be published at home anymore, only when I will have no other choice....

C.S.: One could say then that as long as you haven't been affected directly....

A.B.: But I have been affected all the time. But it does not matter. This is just a difference of perspective. It does not matter how much one suffers for a book, because this is something included in the price one paid for it, it comes with the job. It does not matter that I have no food, it does not matter that I have no ink, that I have no electricity or heat. Nothing matters. All these are exterior factors. The only thing that matters is the book I wrote, it matters whether it is good or not. My physical persona is subordinated to my spiritual persona. If what I produced is good, then everything is fine. If what I produced is not good, then that's something else. I do not like to lament, but this does not mean that I do not know what suffering is, and persecution, and surveillance. But I do not want to talk about it and I do not want to hand them out as reasons, as excuses instead of the value of my own books.

C.S.: *You see, there are moments when history forces us to stop biding our time and take action.*

A.B.: Maybe history will force me to take action, one way or the other. I cannot forecast anything. I don't know what is going to happen in the next five minutes, let alone tomorrow! I do not know what will happen to our country. Maybe I will climb a barricade with a flag in my hand, but I wouldn't want to wear any other clothes than I do right now, be them good or bad. I have told you my simple calculus: I write a book every other four or five years, and so, if I am lucky and live another twenty years of sane life, I can still publish three or four more books. If I am lucky not to grow decrepit. And these books that I might manage to write are very important to me. And I believe that they are at least as useful as those that I already wrote. This is what I think today. It might very well happen that I will find a different situation when I return home and maybe the circumstances will force me to react differently. I do not rule this possibility out, quite on the contrary....

I also have some kind of feeling of disappointment. Why those who talk about Romania present only that face which can be filmed and photographed, but do not x-ray its depths as well? Why this superficiality or indolence, not to use another word? If they really want to do something, to change something, why not examine all the phenomena in depth?

I want to ask you something. A great poet of ours, Nichita Stanescu, lived when Romania was "the most independent", "the most" this... and "the most" that... Why didn't anyone notice him? Wasn't he great enough? It is Romania's fault that did not support him. But, maybe, isn't it also the fault of those who did not look at us, not even by mistake? An African man is attacked in South Africa and, with good reason, everybody feels sorry for the poor unfortunate! A whale is stranded on a beach and again: universal tragedy. But there is something happening with twenty three million people, not to take into account the millions of our neighbours, and there are too few people willing to see what is happening not on the surface, but what is really going on. There are still many things that I need to clear up for myself. But one thing is sure, I have always done what I thought it was more useful. And I did it by giving up a lot of other things, by giving up myself. When I will reach to the conclusion that something else is more useful, then I will do that something. For the time being, I do not see any chances, any help appearing from anywhere. Another example. Romania is a country of French culture and France does not partake in any way to supporting the culture of a people that is so close to it, not even by handing out some books. If they are short-sighted, why should I be as well? Why should I believe that I could be more useful to another people, to another civilisation than to my own people?

C.S.: *A change might come quite soon....*

A.B.: Where? In Romania?

C.S.: *Yes, and I would like for us to sit and talk for a while about the political situation at home.*

A.B.: This is something that I should think about more thoroughly. As I have said before, any change will surely find me with a flag in my hand, on top of a barricade. That barricade where I have been trying to abide for the last two decades.

C.S.: *What about the situation in Transylvania?*

A.B.: Yes, I can talk about that as long as you like. But why do you speak of a change?

C.S.: *Considering the images that I see on television twice a night about what is happening in Romania, it might very well not be "long till far away". How do you see Transylvania's status?*

A.B.: The status decided in 1918... and I don't have anything else to add about it. And I don't even have to.... I think the way the nationality problem was solved in the 1918 declaration was very fare.

C.S.: *Is the Hungarian minority discriminated in Transylvania?*

A.B.: I think it has the same rights and scarcities as we do. Maybe the Hungarians do suffer more because they are a minority, but essentially, the treatment is the same for everybody. If I had one *leu* more than my Hungarian colleague working at the same newspaper, I would be ashamed of that *leu*. The wages are the same, they shop in the same places and walk on the same streets, they suffer of the same cold as us. The situation is the same for everyone. What I mean is that I do not get an additional gram of bread or I do not enjoy more freedom than a Hungarian or a German or a Jew. I do not have any advantages for being Romanian. It is wrong to make such distinctions. There are no advantaged and disadvantaged people. In Romania, we all are a minority right now. Of course that here in the West there are many people writing about Hungarians. Both here and in Hungary. Anyway, Hungarians do have a country of their own. I cannot forget a comment written down by Ciprian Porumbescu in his diary, when he left his native Bucovina: in Hungary, even frogs croak louder. I am joking, of course. But it is better to observe reality from the perspective history forces us to. The dice were rolled for ever with regard to borders.

C.S.: *When you came back from England, you brought me an article from* Times, *that also had a map according to which, in a more distant future, Transylvania will be integrated into Hungary and Bessarabia into Romania.*

A.B.: I brought it to show you an absolutely aberrant thing. I do not understand why Bessarabia, having two thirds of its population Romanians, should be incorporated to Romania, and Transylvania, with three thirds Romanians, should pass to Hungary? Where is the logic? And I also find it absurd for the present borders to change, at least in the next years. It is also true that maybe in ten years from now the borders will be very flexible, will be just symbolic borders. They will not matter any more. But then minority rights will not matter either, because they will be considered in the context of an united Europe.

What I can tell you is that the experts have always been wrong. In the last two months, since I have been here, I have witnessed various events which could not have been predicted a week before. One has to lack the most elementary political sense to believe that in ten years from now Romania will still be as frozen as it is today. It means that one does not take into account that which in the most stereotyped terms is called "the will of the people". This is the outside perspective of people who do not know anything about Romania, who imagine that the world moves around us, that maps are as flexible as a net the spaces of which can be extended or reduced as they please. To me, this looks like a very primitive outlook on history.

I believe that Romania never loses in its run for achieving progress, the better, the more righteous and the new. Romania has always adapted very quickly and then has made some developments which these experts have never been able to predict or understand. I was talking earlier about the 1965 generation, the period right after Stalinism, the Canal, the arrests etc.. I was referring to it as a generation which was capable to recover most of the distances in only five years, to rebuild most of its ties with Europe. And this happened with other occasions as well. In 1916, Romania was nothing but an area around Iasi, and in 1919, it became bigger than it is today.

C.S.: *I too believe in this regeneration power. And maybe it is not a boycott to history, but just a historical sense which makes Romanians wait for the right moment. And maybe that which we call passivity might actually be patience.*

A.B.: Yes, experts do not take into consideration that which has happened in this country in the last one hundred years. In 1876, Eminescu was wondering how could we send to war an army of barefooted. In 1878, we won a war which noone thought we could actually take part in. The same thing happened during World War I. I strongly believe in Romania's recovering and regeneration power. I strongly believe in this star of ours, although it is slow in coming to shine again.

C.S.: *There have been intense discussions with regard to Romania and the fact that it might lose a historic opportunity, a chance that who knows if it will encounter again. Shall we hope again that the last will be the first?*

A.B.: I have great hopes. It doesn't matter. In the 1960s, there have been movements. In 1964, we had the declaration of independence. In 1965, we didn't have any external debts and our neighbours imported from us. Taking these leaps forward into consideration, there are no reasons to doubt anything. Why wouldn't the same thing happen again today? Think about Romanian literature. What was our literature like before the appearance of Eminescu? What was the Romanian language like, what was our way of thinking? Eminescu brought us to Europe, and into the world. And not only Eminescu, but also Titu Maiorescu, Slavici, Caragiale, Creanga. This was a generation that rose from scratch. A generation who brought us on a level with the world. We became like the others, we started thinking and dreaming like the others.

Taking these leaps forward into consideration, what reasons would I have to believe that today the situation is different and that we lost the race. I have no reasons to believe such a thing. On the contrary, I hope that all these experts will be ashamed of their forecasts.

C.S.: *After having spent two months in the West, what do you think about the Romanian exile? What part do you think exile will play in the future?*

A.B.: Oh, God! It would be dishonest to talk about exile because I know very little of it. I formed an image of exile after having read various newspapers, especially in England. Therefore, I don't have a precise image of it. Will it be able to play a part in the future situation? I think it *must*. There are a lot of specialists, a lot of mathematicians, doctors, men of letters who left the country and they should, that is, they have the moral duty to directly or indirectly help their fellow Romanians. It seems to me that they could play a very important part in the future. They managed to integrate themselves into a world where performances and efficiency are at hand, a technological world in which information is not a privilege anymore. They could come back at least as guests to the university departments they had to leave.

C.S.: *And indirectly?*

A.B.: I don't know. By describing to others that we are not at the end of the world.

C.S.: *Tomorrow you are going home.*

A.B.: Yes, and I think I am leaving a little bit changed. I cannot say that I actually changed in only two months, but I got a chance to better see both my good and weak parts. At least I know what I have to do, and how to think. And, no matter what stressing moments are to come from now on, I take for granted all the thoughts I had here, because I had quiet, and I could think, detached from all the stressing factors. I thought myself through, I thought the past and history through. I thought about the future of Romanian literature. I thought about how the novel in general will evolve. What will happen to it? I believe that there will be a time when people will have to turn to themselves. All these informational means, instead of bringing people closer, estrange people from their selves, they do not give them the time to meditate on the way they are, on what it means to be human, these means turn people into robots. It is a different situation than in Romania, but however, they still standardise the people, they serialise them.

C.S.: *But, in order to get to where you want to be, I find this information-through- the-mass-media stage necessary. I think it is a compulsory stage which is missing in Romania.*

A.B.: I understand, but still it hurts. I believe that there should come a time, I don't know when, and I don't know how, but there should come a time when people would turn to themselves, rediscover themselves, analyse themselves. It is impossible for it not to happen, because if it doesn't, then it would be a very sad situation. Therefore, I believe I must consider literature from the perspective of the years to come, starting from this conviction of mine that people will manage to turn to themselves. I keep wondering how will literature be written. In the West, one can hear almost the same comments at all the publishing houses: "People don't read this", "This book is too long", "The unfolding is dragging". It hurts to see this material vision of the soul and art. What is really bad in Romania for instance, is that the theories which are resurfacing, such as the theories about books "for everybody" and other theories with political meaning, well, they are the same in the West as well, they have the same meaning although they are expressed differently. And I think it is a degradation. I suddenly start to get scared when I hear an editor telling me: "Only 200 pages, noone reads more", or "Rapid tempo, because people don't want or get lost in psychological and psychoanalytic theories", or "Too complicated, too alluding". For the last 25 years, I have been hearing nothing else but "for the masses to understand". But people should be raised to the level of art, and not the art lowered to their level. The reasons are different, the civilisations are different, the way of understanding is different, but in essence, it is the same thing.

C.S.: *A famous writer can sometimes impose her/his point of view.*

A.B.: Sure, having reached a certain level of fame, one can impose her/his point of view and the editor will be interested in hearing it, but this idea of "loisir", which gains more and more ground nowadays, is of great interest to me.

I am interested in understanding how we regard history, namely, the sum of events we experienced, and how we should regard it in the future. We need documents of course, we need to know every stage of it, every step we took. What documents do we have about our era?

C.S.: *So, you are probably wondering why did literature have to replace history.*

A.B.: Exactly. Why it had to make up for history, psychology, sociology, philosophy and even for science. Literature was forced to do it. But does it have to surpass this phase of summum or does it have to remain a summum? After all, Shakespeare is the summum of his time, one can find information on meteorology, and physiology, and psychiatry in his work. I studied this particularity in detail. And it is also true for Dostoevski's work.

C.S.: *But in Romania, literature consciously took over other functions as well.*

A.B.: Yes. Surely Shakespeare did not intend to convey other information. It's all about how one makes literature out of life and out of the lived experiences. These are my problems as a writer: how to write literature or how am I supposed to write literature about the time I am experiencing. I think there will be a time when documents will be filed under the denomination "documents", and not under "literature", when sociology will indeed be sociology, when history will really take care of its own business. I have always wondered where will literature go, which will be the standpoints from which man and the era we live in will be looked at.

C.S.: *We might witness interesting mutations, maybe the "Ceausescu epoch" will be intensely documented but in a completely different way.*

A.B.: Probably. It might very well be that the last two decades will become the "obsessing decades". But this will not be enough, we have to overcome these obsessions. What I am mostly interested in is my work. How can I pass over this temporary pain, how can I transform it in an universal human pain, how can I pass over these details which terrorise me today and transform them in details which will always be of interest? It will hurt me so much to find out that in the future I will be judged or that, from everything I wrote, only the truth of a certain moment I experienced will be perceived.

C.S.: *That is, you will be hurt to see that your novels are related to a certain moment.*

A.B.: Exactly. For instance, it would hurt to see *Vanities* regarded as part of the literature of the "obsessing decade", and therefore, limited to certain years.

C.S.: *Or* The Faces of Silence *to be perceived as the collectivisation novel.*

A.B.: It certainly is not the collectivisation novel. As much as *Refuges* or *The Way of the Ash are not* the novels of "the obsessing present". This is my wish: for them *not to be* that. I want to go *beyond* this reality.

C.S.: *I think it is so, because for instance, your last novel can also be understood, for many reasons, as the novel of the impotence of writing. It is the novel about the way in which an intellectual succeeds or not to accomplish himself. I think it is a novel that is not related to any precise moment.*

A.B.: This is exactly what I intended, this is how I would like it to be understood. That is why it bothers me when I hear people talking about my so-called courage. How will this courage matter tomorrow? It will not matter at all. How will the events which today are hindering me from my writing be of value tomorrow? I am interested to know whether I am indeed writing literature or not. I am interested to know whether my work is good or not. This is the way I wish to be judged, because this is the way I judge myself. Did I or didn't I write good literature? That's it.

C.S.: *You want to be as good of a writer in year 2000 and in the future as well.*

A.B.: A better writer. That is the reason why I have always resumed certain themes which I thought were not fulfilled from a literary point of view. I think that the love novel has never come out the way I wish it did. Therefore, I have stubbornly resumed it, hoping that one day I would succeed in writing it the way I feel it should be written. For the time being, I still have a feeling of incomplete regarding this topic. There are a lot of themes which are crucial today, but which will not be of interest tomorrow anymore if they won't be true literature, and not history, sociology, or reportage. Think of a book about the most aberrant hunger or about a strike: I wouldn't really care about reading it. For instance, there is this author who turned the world upside down, I am talking about Solzhenitsyn. Do you still read *The Gulag Archipelago* with the same interest you did when it came out? I am not making a statement. I am asking a question. These are my own questions about the era I live in.

A writer has a duty to take out of the historic events those universal human truths which are everlastingly valid. Literature must surpass the photographic transcription of reality, its hyper-realist description, that is, literature must give them other meanings as well, it must elevate them to a symbolic, metaphoric level. I am interested to look upon our era from this perspective, and to try to consider it, for instance, from the perspective of the year 2000. I try to examine myself, the person I am today, with the eyes of the person I will be. Of course that I wrote, I wrote a lot, about this era, but especially in my last novels I tried and I still try to find those elements which are understood today and will also be understood tomorrow. I want to skip the day when the book was written. Thus, I know, I think I know, which are my good and bad parts. And I mostly thought about what I should do. I surely do not separate the man from the writer, the political being inside myself from the writer. And I cannot but remain a political being. But I did understand, more than ever, that literature must ask questions, not give answers. And now it is very clear to me which are the questions that I have to ask myself and to shout them out loud.

C.S.: *The questions that you will ask.*

A.B.: Yes, the questions that I *will ask*. I know exactly what is bad in Romania, but I also discovered what is bad here. I am not referring to politics and to society, but to the man as a psycho-social entity, to man in general. Because, after all, Romanians are different from the people here. I thought about man in general. Which is the face of evil, on both sides. And which is the face of good, of course. During my stay here, in the West, I have been thinking that I paid too much attention to politics, and not that much attention to the spirit and, as a writer, in the following years, I will have to put politics on the second place. And also because I have an age which forces me to do what I must do, and not what I want to do, what I think I can and am ready to do. For the Great Confrontation: with myself and with my own limits.

C.S.: *You are going home tomorrow and you still haven't told me why your novels are optimistic....*

A.B.: Their optimism comes from my blind trust in this darn life! And this darn nation.

München, December 1989

Post-script

Fifteen years passed since the interview. Many, rapid years. But I did not forget anything about the interview, and I still intensely feel even the temperature of that evening. And I wish that my good friend, Crisula Stefanescu, would have misplaced the interview among her papers and books for another fifteen years. I have never exposed my wounds the way they were. Because I have never expected anything in return, neither "my country's gratitude", nor someone else's understanding or admiration. As regards my convictions, I couldn't have changed them, which is something I hope those who will have the curiosity to read this text might discover. Yesterday, like today, no matter what the consequences and the contexts are, I said and wrote exactly what it seemed moral and correct to me, in conformity with my own convictions, because, as Montaigne said: "We do not have to play our part in this world in order to dazzle others but for ourselves, there, inside, where no other eyes but ours can penetrate."

Thus, I used to write out of a need to feel free and not in order to be considered courageous, because I did not believe in courage, and my texts from that time bring plenty of proof that I tried to avoid this attribute. "No other virtue is easier to imitate than courage", thought Vladimir Jankelevitch. "Any ethics of courage should begin with a picture of its parodies." And in Romania, parodies have always found fantastic launching ramps. The price for leaving this comfortable zone was, and unfortunately it still is, very difficult to bear. If I were to be totally honest, for me, this price has the name of two somewhat related feelings: disgust and uselessness, feelings which, despite the time that has passed from the Revolution, have not lost in intensity. On the contrary, parodies have annulled true courage. Nothing was left complete, unstained. Unfortunately, today, both Mount Everest and *Dealul Morii* (The Hill of the Mill) have the same height and importance, they are both mountains. And, as Sainte-Beuve used to say, Caliban pretends to be Shakespeare and almost noone notices it, or even worse, noone knows the truth. The *calibans* appear periodically, like the seeds of Camus' plague. And after the revolution, just like after World War II, it has been their era. And the people today, just like those yesterday, are not all that surprised and, after a while, they do not recognise the *calibans* anymore. Then, naturally, they disappear into ridicule.... However, generally speaking, the most beautiful slogans and ideas are taken over precisely by those who did not fight for them, and who do not understand them, those who had fled from any kind of confrontation. I sincerely regret the fact that I had to confess the names of those two feelings that I experience so often, but nothing of what happens today urges me to use euphemisms. The pains, the fears and the questions noted down by Cris Stefanescu in those days of great ordeal and concern make reference to a world which awaits a rightful remembering in studies, novels, or in any type of evocations. Because, if we do not know what it was like and what was hard about it, it is difficult to understand the world we live in with its abnormal psychologies and, of course, it is difficult to understand history's movements, which are sometimes slow, barely perceivable, and other times rapid, sudden. History: violent, harsh, it mercilessly struck a world lacking the sense of tragedy, a world where, like in magical rituals, the unknown or the unperceived were denied, where everything was negotiated, a world where one of the tutorial gods was "this will do". After many years of long and tormenting benumbing, after time had stood still for so long, finally, there we were, in an important and solemn turning point in history, in a space between fear and hope, and nevertheless, noone believed that very soon communism was really going to fall down.

I still do not have enough words for the anxiety I felt in those days when I knew and saw that the dice had been decisively rolled, when I was afraid of both the world that had to die and the world that was about to be born, because in that strange agony, on the borderline between those two worlds, nothing could have been kept under control, as the hatred and the joy of our fellow men seemed equally dangerous. These peculiar attitudes seemed vital to me also due to the fact that they had to take their appropriate place in a novel, because the unexpected, the new, the unusual could have shown their most interesting sides at any time. And such a turning point of intricate change, when everything was new, was forcing my memory and observation spirit to the utmost because my destiny was at stake, my destiny not only as a writer but also as a humble human being. In the books I had written up to that point, I was interested in man's relation to history, to a brutal, overwhelming history. I was tempted to say an unfair history, but I gave that attribute up: history is quite in the likeliness of those who accept it or confront it. I was also interested in life in concentration camps, in the faces of terror and, of course, in the two vital pulses: love and death during terror. I had written a lot of articles about mental death, an infamous face of death, and suddenly I had the chance to witness a change which I had been intensely desired without believing it was possible to take place in my lifetime. I found it vital as well, for it made one truly feel what was it like not to be watched, not to have to whisper, not to be held responsible for what one said etc. However, as a writer, I could not have written if I had not freed myself from these constraints. I strongly believe, and I keep saying it, that we are our books. Nobody forgives you for what you did not do or could not have done. When having a book analysed, the context in which it was written does not matter at all, and neither do the sufferings, the joys or the shortages, namely, all which could happen to you during your lifetime. You exist through that bit of eternity that you managed to entrust the paper with. That's it. And this is what I stubbornly believed during that interview, although, in reality, I knew that at that time answering to a few questions which were waiting and which could not have been postponed was more important than any theory about novels and literature in general. What was I going to do with my life? I could not ignore all that I had written, all that I had shouted through literature, with those literary means I had had at my disposal. However, although the paid price was big, history claimed much more and, moreover, it did not grant you the certainty that it would evolve in the direction you and the rest of the world wished for, but it imperatively requested an answer from each and everyone of us. And it is a well-known thing that there are lots of answers to that inevitable "*where to?*" And each answer/tendency could have been exemplified by a lot of examples, some of which were convincing. Many of my fellow writers got lost in formal exercises - writing above everything else -, reactivating or imitating stranded tendencies of the West. Others could have peacefully lived outside history, making comments about the weather and performing pirouettes of refined intellectuals: *today I read two verses by Virgil* etc.. While most of them were paying their unworthy "mite", hoping that thus their "work" would be saved. And the number of those who openly admitted to be scared was not to be ignored. There were of course just a few people who took the risk of looking truth straight in the eye and of saying that which deserved to be told in those terrible times. However, not even those people came up with some "future plans": what were we going to do afterwards....? The answer, obeying our good old tradition, was easy: *What are we going to do afterwards....? We'll see then. We'll see afterwards....* And this answer covers up fumbling and anxiety. It is also true that it was very hard to truly think about victory. About an immediate victory. After the Revolution, I certainly found out that the number of the courageous and of the prestigious people was huge, but this is another story. Anyways, the answer requested by those moments is to be found inside ourselves. One can only be free when succeeds in overcoming fear, in accepting that anything could happen, even death. And in the last years of the dictatorship, this is one hypothesis that could not have been ruled out. At that time, the 'drawer' literature, another idea that had started to develop, seemed to me an unknown deposit that could not have been accessed precisely when it was greatly needed. It was clear that it existed only as an excuse for fear and powerlessness. Who could have known when were the days for "opening the drawers" to come and if our fellow men of that time would still be needing them? Censorship and the *Securitate* were just massive excuses for cowards. People knew from the beginning *what was working and what was not working* and most of them were hiding under their covers. As for me, I said and I did exactly what I thought fitted me, and today I have no doubt that reason and the data I had at that important turning point were defeated - then and now as well - by my immense power of deceiving myself believing that people could be *different*, that they will be *different* after the disappearance of the stressing factors. And as regards these factors.... I knew my *Securitate* agents, I used to meet them almost every day, "by accident": at exhibition openings, at the theatre or at various events where there were lots of people present. They used to appear out of the blue when I was with my best friends, they would hug me and, in front of my friends, they would promise me things that they knew I was lacking - better cigarettes, various food products -, while other men, by accident, had their photo cameras with them. On one hand, they were trying to intimidate me, and on the other hand, they were trying to arouse my colleagues' distrust, to show the others that I had good relations with that institution and that I received help, which could have been credible given those living conditions when poverty had reached an unimaginable degree. No matter how hard I tried, I still do not have enough words to describe the repulsion and the anxiety that I felt each day, the physical and psychological exhaustion accompanied by the terrible embarrassment of having been forced to hunt for food from morning till night, to humiliate myself in front of all the butchers and restaurant keepers, to beg for a few hundred *lei* to the big hot-shots in the economic department of the Writers' Union....

"Is there life before death?" was one of the questions most frequently heard almost in all social strata. Having constantly been in the attention of that sinister institution, I could never know when they would move from threat to action. Were there people who had been exposed to too much radiation, or was it just a rumour meant to intimidate us? The foreign radio stations kept talking about this method which had been used on the protestors in Brasov, and about other intimidation methods as well, which had been used on some people who had "illegally" founded an union, not to mention the rumours about the strange fate of the miners' leaders in Valea Jiului. I could not believe in betrayals - the way they were unfortunately disclosed after the Revolution - because that did not suit me. Therefore, there was only one question awaiting to be answered: were those miners really inured "by accident", those miners whose claims could have been published even in *Scanteia* given the conditions at that time? A sole tragic certainty: a man had been killed in prison for political reasons - Gheorghe Ursu. Were those psychiatric treatments that everybody talked about really used? Weren't the people admitted in hospitals really sick? My psychiatric colleagues and friends answered differently to this question, although in those times one was tempted to believe the worst. I myself met once a paraphrenic, pitied by some international associations, who had not only political claims but also other claims, such as the prohibition of church bells because their ringing, at certain precise times and in certain circumstances, were phonically polluting Cluj. Due to the fact that the press could only praise the historic, or epoch-making successes, the rumour was sovereign. Thus, besides certain truths, there were both professional misinformers and many amateurs willing to immediately spread around any aberration. And it was difficult to find your way in this space where gossiping, "puttering" and having an opinion about everything without having the slightest previous documentation are sports with an ancient tradition. No matter how rational and lucid you might have been, something of those rumours would still stay in your subconscious, a little something that emphasised the anxiety, and the hypothesis that not even the biggest danger should be ruled out, given the fact that the *Securitate* agents would not stop "warning" us that something was made ready for us, something bad of course. It is also true that I never refused to talk to them, because I could discover the best solutions to protect myself only by knowing them, by deciphering from our discussions what they knew and they did not know about me, by grasping their questions and threats, sometimes violent, other times insinuated. During a failed attempt to organise my stuff after some thieves had broken into my house a few months before and, probably having been disappointed by not having found any money or jewellery, had scattered my books and manuscripts all over the place, I found a note dated May 1989, in which I had written down all the rumours that were circulating about me: "I was severely bitten and I was in the hospital. I was of course bitten because of what I had written in *The Way of The Ash*. The price of the book at the flee market in Cluj: 1,000 *lei* / copy. 150 *lei* for borrowing it to read it, 200 *lei* reading it / xerox copy. My novel had been taken off the market. I had my papers done to leave the country for good. I am a *Securitate* agent, that is why I was allowed to have the novel published. I am dying. One night, when I was coming back home, a group of tramps disfigured me. I am a homosexual. I am a womaniser. I will be transferred to the local paper. Etc. Therefore, by no means do I have to be what I am. In addition, the readers' reactions are tested and not a single day passes without my finding out something new of this vast repertoire. It all reached the point where not even my sister believed me when I told her by the phone that I was fine. And for all this nagging to never stop, I was summoned to the Commissariat to be sent to a military unit." And I even recorded various sensations in order to better reflect the atmosphere of that time: "At a food store in Cluj, women's underwear are sold and it is compulsory to also buy two kilograms of oceanic fish along with the underwear. Telling this piece of news to a friend who also likes this kind of curiosities, he replied with another one, even weirder: in town B., one cannot get a coffin anymore unless, in addition to the paid price, she/he does not also give a hundred eggs and does not buy a wig as well! Someone was telling me the other day that at a pigs farm nearby Bucharest, there are a lot of horribly crippled animals: hungry people, gipsies, guards etc., they all just cut joints of meat off the living animals. Of course surrealism has appeared in literature in Romania too, I wrote at that time, but I wouldn't have thought that I was going to discover it in everyday life as well." And in July 1989, in order to reflect the atmosphere even better, I wrote a few things down thinking that this kind of "moments" might become part of a novel: "The same guy with a mustache accompanies me everywhere in Bucharest: to the park, on the street, he waits for me when I leave from the family Boeras.... But one evening when I returned to my hotel I had the courage to ask him what he wanted from me: «These days, it's better not to walk alone all day long!», he laughed!". At that time I also made a note out of a phone warning I had received: "If you make a move, if you do like others did before, you're dead!". Was it a *Securitate* agent? Was it a telltale? Was it someone's stupid idea of a joke? A close friend of mine, employed in the upper levels of the regime, once whispered to me about a plan to do all those who had influence on the masses in. Therefore, who could make out the difference between truth, lie and intimidation at that time? Who to believe? Sure I could discover the signs of their presence everywhere, their permanent strive to intimidate me, to demonstrate me that they knew all my moves. But precisely the fact that I was so vulnerable, that they could have done what ever they wanted to me at any moment, helped me overpass my fear, and do only what seemed morally compulsory to me. As it is often the case, offence was the best weapon. The situation was similar to the relationship one has with death, from a certain age onwards: one accepts that death is inevitable, that it can arrive at any moment, that it is not an idea, as Alain used to say, it is important to be aware of it, not to call it through fear and despair, but to fill with facts and life that space in our souls which death will forever take hold of when the time will come. Therefore, I did the impossible, and I behaved in a very normal way, I wrote as if I lived in the freest of the countries, I forced them to believe that something was missing from their data, and especially I forced them to believe that I was not alone.

And I successfully played this role of the very self-confident guy, who was also very sure of his relationships in Romania and especially abroad, relationships unknown to the *Securitate*. This was actually the only possible role - besides those very common roles of fleeing, of coward complicity or of selfish collaboration -, a role that it was very difficult to deviate from without the most unexpected consequences. As the enemy, you were treated if not with respect, at least with more caution, while as a simple collaborator or as a person brought on the good path again, you became some kind of slave worthy of disdain. Being something else, being something different from what they thought you were meant losing. I recall that a censorship super-boss with many stars on his shoulder asked me to give up almost 180 pages of one of my novels. After a long, tormenting bargaining that lasted a few months, after endless threats, withdrawals, returns, only 78 lines were still rasing discussions. With the risk of not having the book published, I did not want to give those lines up either. Other negotiations followed, of course, different versions, reciprocal obstinacies and, when it seemed that there was no way out, the censorship guy held out his hand and told me - I do not know whether out of conviction or not: “Very well, sir, we can leave it like it is. You would have disappointed my if you had given up!”. Elegant exit? The consequence of the aforementioned role? The same thing used to happen in everyday life as well. "Even if I stumble one day on a rock, fell down and break my leg or my neck because I'm clumsy," I used to assure colonel O., "you would still be seen guilty!" Stimulated by the interview, I am disclosing all these things after so many years, *now when the events and the clenches of that time matter only* for the two interlocutors. It seems like I am talking about a person whose power of disillusioning himself and whose candour move me, especially today when everything is clear, when all the classifications have been made. We know with great accuracy who are the true democrats, the true freedom fighters, the dissidents and the people who resisted it all, including the *Securitate* and the censorship. There is a list and a hierarchy of the cultured and the subtle. I finally find out exactly who are the most and the least clever, with who and from what year, month and day does our literature begin, who deserves a Nobel and who deserves to be forgotten. There is a geography of the wounds and a hierarchy of the great ailing, but there is still one hierarchy missing, that of the imposture and of the shamelessness, a list which is impossible to make now or, I believe, neither in the years to come. Could people have imagined back then that a time of illumination would come? Could they have imagined that the majority of those who did all the hard work would be guilty of having done something, of having taken risks or having tried to be a par with the rest of the world? By the way, I do not unfortunately see any difference between that which the *Securitate* agents and the party activists understood and that which many of the people today understand, some of which are young and pretend to have read the books of my generation. The lack of culture, the lack of a sense of reality and of history are amazing. While the old activists, who were denying these books, were defending their positions, the new *calibans* want to have a position, they want to be in the first rows of culture using exactly the same means as the others did. Who could have imagined that today, just like yesterday, even the political orientation, be it in a continuous change like the times, would often be a substitute for books? Just like in a world, where one can contact any other spot on the planet in a matter of seconds, but those who should always *communicate*, who should truly *know*, act as if they were more isolated than the Aborigines. How many times, in various contexts, did I find myself feeling obsessed with the ironical connotation of the Eminescu's verses: "We each do our place retain / As we were, some remain."[1] But let's return to the atmosphere of those times.

I was supposed to go to the usual meeting of the Gulliver Group in Amsterdam and, at the same time, I had another two invitations: one from a department in the Ministry of Foreign Affairs, in England, and from the University of Heidelberg, from professor Klaus Heitmann, whose department the critic Sami Damian was part of. Some of my friends either advised me not to leave or they even obstinately condemned me, telling

---

[1] Translation by Corneliu M. Popescu

me that I felt like travelling abroad exactly when our villages and churches were being destroyed, when there were so many miseries taking place, which were revealing the true face of the Ceausescu regime etc. They said that I was leaving in order to show that there was still possible to travel.... For the watchful people, leaving the country was as suspect as not leaving it. Generally speaking, the suspects are *the others*.... Those who were condemning me so vehemently had memory problems: unlike myself, they had travelled all around the world, during the golden age too, during the Ceausescu regime as well, they had been delayed in the West for as long as they had wanted to. In addition to the fact that finally I had the chance to know what I had been wanting to for such a long time, the projects of the Gulliver Group in Amsterdam seemed very interesting to me, as regards the dialogue with the East European intellectuals, the tangible measures that were to be taken, things which I could not have talked about without the risk of having been misinterpreted in conformity with the good old Bucharest tradition. One year ago, in my book *The Temptation of Waste*, I actually published the text which was read when the group was founded in 1987.However, above all this was my need to get out of that tormenting environment, to look at myself from the outside and to think about my true job. As man of scientific formation, I could not live from one page to the next, I had made a lifelong plan, which could not have been thoroughly accomplished without a lot of information, without readings and permanent contacts with what was thought and written abroad. Therefore, reconnecting myself to the world was extremely necessary at a time when everything seemed turned into stone in Romania: a bizarre island outside time, two characters, the same recital, a concentration camp where each and every one of us looked for individual surviving solutions, where night, fear and hunger were the masters dictating the rules. And where I suspected that there were a lot of good people under this massive layer of darkness, many intellectuals who were thinking Romania's spiritual map of tomorrow, prepared to *build* that which had not been possible during communism, to close the ranks in the name of a better future which we thought that we deserved after so many years of suffering. A future for which I had always felt that I had to do more, I had to be better prepared than I knew myself to have been. Having been specialised in understanding the human mind and its pathology, I certainly did not find it difficult to suspect the hatred that was to come when all the barriers were to be removed, the revolt of the cultural periphery, the attack of the slums of the spirit. But what happened next surpassed any of my expectations, both in intensity and duration. However, back then at the end of 1989, I was still dreaming - together with those close to me with whom I was thinking about solutions -, I was not only dreaming of the disappearance of that long, totalitarian night, but I was greedily gathering indispensable information. What were people writing about, who was writing, what were the most discussed issues in literature and many other similar questions were part of my painful obsessions at that time. Obsessions which, unfortunately, I had to keep to myself, because the agony of communism had reached paroxysm and all the people that I was meeting were contaminated by politics, they were living it at full intensity, which was actually *the right intensity for that great turning point.*

Thus, I left for Germany with an aching feeling that I was not coming back anymore or, more precisely, that I would not be allowed into the country anymore, as I had been told many times not only by those who had given me my passport, but also by other important people who seemed to know everything about me and who had advised me to stay, which was an unconceivable idea to me. Therefore, the first thing I did when I arrived in Munich was to look for some networks to illegally enter the country. This is something I had never confessed to anyone, not even to my friends, Crisula and Andi Stefanescu, for fear that I would be considered ridiculous, at least ridiculous. Many Romanians dreamed about and risked their lives fleeing from Romania, while I would have paid the same price trying to come back to Romania. Anyway, I spent a lot of time with the people waiting in small hotels in Munich to receive asylum, I analysed all my options, the way these people arrived in Germany, the price they paid. Because everything had a price bigger than the success guarantees. During those weeks I examined not only the possibilities of clandestinely entering Romania, but also what could I do if I were sent back from the border or caught during my attempt to return home. After reaching my first certainties, I continued my trip to Heidelberg, and from there to Holland, France and England.

It was probably the most complicated journey of my life, an inner trip against fear, cowardice, death. Because, no matter how many things you know about freedom, dignity, courage, future, you find out their true measure, their true taste only when you have to express them, and to defend them, only when reality forces you to ascertain yourself through taking action. Then, you learn exactly who you are, and this can be revealed only by the grave sound of that action you have to take. By being there and meeting people who in their own way were influencing history, I realised that my pain was far greater than I thought it was, both my pain and my anxiety. And, in a strange way, I had not know the necessary words to express them, because I had thoroughly convinced myself that the people I had met, the friends, the future friends and the strangers did not know the dimensions of our fears and pains, I had convinced myself that the world was not divided only between the good and the bad. The deeper I was going into the West, the more I felt at home and I was trying to live in the future, in that which was going to happen soon, I was trying to picture it with those data I had and which were worrying me. What I mean is that even the future freedom seemed to me accompanied by fears, greater fears than those I had experienced before. In those days, I had the incredible chance to see the Wall of Berlin fall down and, on my entire journey back, I was haunted by a fantastic scene: the pianist who, nearby the wall, was madly playing in its shadow, while cranes, excavators, regular people were trying to destroy it or to just look from its top, from the most painful and absurd building, to look at the other side, the free side of a country which could not have borne anymore the excruciating reality, the absurdness of history. When I was in London I held the microphone of a radio station which I had piously listened to for years: BBC. Therefore, I could tell uncensored what I thought, given the fact that I did not care what would the consequences of my gesture upon my return be. But I did not want to be more courageous abroad, I did not want to say more things than I had already done at home. I had the same conviction during my dialogue with Crisula Stefanescu. Maybe it is time to say that, all throughout my trips in the West, the family Stefanescu was a compulsory landmark. My good friend Anneli Ute Gabanyi, before leaving "Europa Libera", assured me that she left me in good hands and that her successor at the Research Department of the radio station, Crisula Stefanescu, was very competent professionally and also a fine person. Time and various circumstances utterly proved her right. In the Stefanescu household I met or saw again many outstanding exile personalities. There, I was finding out not only the latest important political news but also the sports news or any other type of news. The idea of having a dialogue which Andi Stefanescu was going to record somewhat surprised me, because we had thoroughly examined all those issues so many times before that I did not see what else I could add, but I immediately accepted the offer. After having read this dialogue today, I am amazed by the calm and certainty of that time. My thoughts were directed towards my home country: I did not want to miss the inevitable Event which had shaken our sad East. And Romania, of course, could not make an exception, could not and it was impossible to be avoided. I was returning home with a great, anticipated certainty, but, when I told some of my friends about it, they thought I was out-of-place or even instigating. However, I was not surprised by their reaction: thousands of justifications and excuses can always be found for cowardice and ignorance. I was lucky that, in a few days time, that which had to happen really took place, history payed a visit to us too, and asked for its ratio of blood, hopes and illusions.

Augustin Buzura
Bucharest, 10 July 2004

Augustin Buzura (born on 22nd of September 1938), one of the most representative novelists of the post war Romanian literature, was a member of the Romanian Academy, president of the Romanian Cultural Institute from its coming into being till January 17th 2005. His editorial debut was in 1963 with the short stories volume entitled *The Cape of Good Hope*, The Publishing House for Literature. Other published volumes: *Why does the eagle fly?* (short stories, The Publishing House of Youth, 1966), *The Absentees* (novel, The Dacia Printing House, 1970, The Writers Union Award), *Faces of Silence* (novel, The Romanian Book Printing House, 1974, The Writers Union Award), *Prides* (novel, Dacia Printing House, 1977, The Romanian Academy Award), *The Voices of the Night* (novel, The Romanian Book Printing House, 1980, the Writers Union Award), *Refuges* (novel, the Romanian Book Printing House, 1984), *The Grey Road* (novel, the Romanian Book Printing House, 1988), *Requiem for fools and beasts* (novel, The Universe Printing House, 1999).

Crisula Stefanescu (born on 1949) graduated from the University of Bucharest, Faculty of Philology. In 1982 she moved abroad. From 1983 till 1995 she worked as an editor and as an analyst and scholar for the "Free Europe" radio station in Munchen. We mention the following volumes out of the published ones: *The spell of the Hour* (poems, The Literary Diary Printing House, Bucharest, 1998), *Signs* (poems, The Albatross Printing House, Bucharest, 1999), *Ana and the Satan* (five acts play, The Literary Diary Printing House, Bucharest, 1999). She has also signed a great number of translations and interviews